SAVED

SAV

SAVED

RESCUED ANIMALS AND THE LIVES THEY TRANSFORM

TEXT BY
Karin Winegar

PHOTOGRAPHS BY
Judy Olausen

FOREWORD BY
Dr. Jane Goodall

PREFACE BY
Dr. Temple Grandin

Da Capo

LIFE LONG

A MEMBER OF
THE PERSEUS BOOKS GROUP

Copyright © 2008 by Karin Winegar and Judy Olausen
Foreword copyright © 2008 by Jane Goodall
Preface copyright © 2008 by Temple Grandin
All photographs by Judy Olausen

Designed by Pauline Neuwirth, Neuwirth & Associates, Inc.
Set in 11 point Spectrum by the Perseus Books Group

Library of Congress Cataloging-in-Publication Data

Winegar, Karin.
Saved : rescued animals and the lives they transform / text by Karin Winegar ; photographs by Judy Olausen ; foreword by Jane Goodall ; preface by Temple Grandin. —1st Da Capo Press ed.
p. cm.
ISBN 978-0-7382-1276-0 (alk. paper)
1. Pets—Anecdotes. 2. Animal rescue—Anecdotes.
3. Human-animal relationships—Anecdotes. I. Title.
SF416.W56 2008
636.08'32—dc22
2008020616

First Da Capo Press edition 2008

Published by Da Capo Press
A Member of the Perseus Books Group
www.dacapopress.com

Da Capo Press books are available at special discounts for bulk purchases in the United States by corporations, institutions, and other organizations. For more information, please contact the Special Markets Department at the Perseus Books Group, 2300 Chestnut Street, Suite 200, Philadelphia, PA 19103, or call (800) 810-4145, ext. 5000, or e-mail special.markets@perseusbooks.com.

10 9 8 7 6 5 4 3 2 1

For the animals.
—KW

To my husband, Brian Sundstrom, for his kindness, grace,
understanding, and patience.
And to my two beautiful and smart stepchildren,
Aricka and Bjorn Sundstrom.
—JO

CONTENTS

SAVED

FOREWORD

By Dr. Jane Goodall

SAVED IS AN inspired collection of real-life stories about rescued animals and the people who rescue them. When I received the manuscript, with a letter asking if I would consider writing an introduction, I at once decided that it would be impossible—I was deeply involved in writing a book of my own. I simply had no time to write anything else. Yet I glanced through the chapters anyway. As the days went by, some of the stories haunted me, and ideas and phrases suitable for an introduction came, unbidden, into my mind. Surely, said a still, small voice, you can make just a little time to help launch this moving book. And so, after all, I found myself agreeing to write these words.

The stories are especially compelling because they are not only about abandoned, abused, and tortured animals—Karin Winegar and her photographer, Judy Olausen, also care deeply about the extraordinary collection of dedicated people, often bruised and hurting themselves, who have become guardians of the oppressed. Above all the book is about the relationship between animals and people. As the rescued animals begin to respond to care and respect, and to what may be the first gentle petting they have ever known, so their human rescuers are comforted—even transformed—by those they have saved. As I read the stories, my eyes often filled with tears; the next moment I was smiling through them.

I well know the healing power of animals. A few years ago, I went to visit a remarkable and very brave ten-year-old boy, Donny, who was dying of cancer. It had been one of his last wishes to meet Jane Goodall. A few months after his death, I called his mother to find out how the family was coping. She told me that Jesse, Donny's younger brother, was inconsolable. He was deeply depressed, he was not eating properly, and he was doing very badly at school.

"Trouble is, Donny was here at home for the last few years of his life," she told me. "He had so many treatments we couldn't get him to school. So the two boys became very, very close."

"Do you have a dog?" I asked. No, they didn't. I said that I felt sure that Jesse needed a dog.

"My husband won't have one," she explained. I asked if I could speak to him, and I spent ten minutes trying, unsuccessfully it seemed, to convince him. Saddened, I hung up.

And then, several weeks later, I received a glowing letter of thanks from Jesse—and a photo of him, beaming, pressed close against a golden brown and white mutt named Spike. I also received a letter from his mother describing how, after all, my words had made a difference, how they had gone together to the shelter, and how Jesse and Spike had instantly known each other. Jesse arrived in time to rescue the abandoned Spike, and the dog was there to start healing Jesse's hurting heart. A year later, I met the whole family (except for Spike), and they told me it was not just Jesse who had benefited from Spike, but the entire family. They had probably saved him from euthanasia: in return he had brought comfort to all their lives with his unconditional love.

Increasingly, around the world, the therapeutic power of animals is being recognized. People living with loved pets tend to get sick less often and to live longer than those with no animals in their lives. There is scientific evidence that proves, beyond doubt, that the presence of a dog, cat, or other friendly and gentle animal can bring about psychological changes, such as a lowering of blood pressure. Stroke victims make new efforts to move semi-paralyzed limbs in order to stroke a friendly animal. More and more hospitals and nursing homes are allowing—even encouraging—

visits from "therapy" animals. Autistic children and others with learning disabilities often make great strides in reading skills when the listener is a friendly, uncritical dog.

Perhaps the first-ever official therapy dog was a little white stray who became a resident at a large children's hospital in London in the early 1900s. He had no owner and no home and had clearly known great hardship before the hospital staff adopted him. Once there, he always sought out the sickest children and would curl up on their beds. When a hygiene inspector threw up his hands in horror and banned the little white dog, death rates increased. Indeed, the increase was so marked that the hospital allowed him back.

I was in New York with Mary Lewis, my administrative assistant and friend, at the time of the terrorist attacks of 9/11. The city, for the first few days (before fear and anger took over), was in total shock. People were numb and dazed. On the second day, Mary and I came upon a woman walking near our hotel with a very small and very lively dog called Kisses. We were crouched down in a trice, petting and having our faces licked. And we were not alone in desperately needing what we call a "dog fix." It was heartwarming to see frozen faces break into smiles as people bent down to pet the little creature, so full of love and doggy kisses. She must have helped many that day—just one more example of what animals can do for us.

It is one of the great tragedies that everywhere, in every country, there are millions of abused, hurting, frightened, and sick animals—dogs and cats, horses, birds, and so many more. Animals domesticated to the service of man and horribly betrayed.

Karin has sought out examples of people who sacrifice a great deal to help these suffering animals. So compelling is her writing that the personalities of both the animals and humans become very real—I feel as if I have actually met some of them. And Judy's sensitive and revealing photographs bring the text even more vividly to life. Indeed, this book is the result of a perfect partnership—the collaboration of two people who care passionately about animals but who care about people too. And who are able, through their respective gifts of lucid writing and perceptive photography, to share their passion with others. I had tea with them in Minnesota in the spring, and I could feel the power of their combined determination to make a difference.

I hope that *Saved* will help all those dogs and cats who languish in shelters, and all the other abandoned, beaten, and frightened animals who are suffering at human hands. And that more old people in more retirement homes will be visited, and more often, by therapy animals. That more prisons will set up programs that allow inmates to train guide dogs or care for homeless animals. That more hospitals will include visiting hours for those four-legged friends that can motivate the sick to make the effort to carry on living, and bring peace and comfort to those who have reached the end of their time on earth.

Most people will be shocked to read of the acts of cruelty to animals taking place across the American continent—things that most people do not know about, and even if they do, feel there is nothing they can do about it. These stories will not only raise awareness, but I hope will also encourage everyone to do their bit to help. Few people will want to turn their houses or yards into animal rescue centers—and only some people have the passion and courage and temperament to take on such a project. But everyone who cares can do something. Help to spread awareness, volunteer at a rescue center, write letters, make donations, raise money. And if you are thinking of sharing your life with an animal, for goodness' sake rescue one from a shelter. Don't buy one, especially from a puppy mill or pet shop. My own life has been enriched by a long succession of rescued dogs. How rewarding they have been.

WHEN I WAS three and a half, I had no speech and all the full-blown symptoms of severe autism. Back in 1949, most doctors recommended sending severely autistic children to an institution. Fortunately my mother persevered and found a nanny who worked every day with me for many hours.

The teenage years were the worst years of my life. I was constantly teased and called names like "retard," "workhorse," and "bones." Lunchtime in the cafeteria and walking across the parking lot were torture. When I was fourteen, I was kicked out of a large girls' school for throwing a book at a girl who called me names.

My mother found a wonderful, special boarding school that had a farm and horses. When I was with the horses, it was a refuge from the teasing. The kids who were the worst teasers were not interested in riding horses or milking the cows.

During a long career, I have observed that some of the people who are most skilled at working with animals are not the super social types who just want to engage in idle chitchat. They are the loners, the people who are kind of different. Today some of these dedicated animal people would be diagnosed as having Asperger's Syndrome, which is a mild form of autism, dyslexia, or learning difficulty. In fact, many famous scientists, artists, and musicians from the past would be diagnosed with Asperger's or dyslexia if they were alive today. It is the people who are a bit different who accomplish many wonderful things.

I could never understand why some people deny animal consciousness until I learned that my thinking was very different. I think in pictures, like Google for images. During my thirties, I figured out that most people think mainly in words, a fact I learned by conducting a series of interviews. I asked the same test question over and over to many different people: "Access your memory of church steeples; how does this information come into your mind?" Most people see a vague, generalized, generic steeple, whereas I see specific identifiable individual steeples. They flash up sequentially in my mind like a series of slides. It was a great insight to find out that other people have less specific thinking.

To understand animals you have to get away from thinking in words. You have to think in pictures or use one of the other senses such as sound or touch. It is sensory-based thinking, not word-based. It is often the most verbal thinkers who deny animals' true consciousness.

For me, language narrates the images that pop into my imagination. According to some philosophers, I would not be truly conscious. Visual and sensory-based thinking is a continuum, and some people have more sensory-based thinking than others. Brain-scan research is starting to verify that people on the autism spectrum think with the visual part of the brain more than non-autistic people. This new research has given me valuable insight into the fact that different people have different ways of thinking. Many individuals on the autism spectrum relate well to animals. Therapeutic horseback-riding programs help autistic individuals of all ages. Several mothers have told me that their non-verbal child started talking when he or she started riding horses.

I related to many of the stories in *Saved* about how animals and people with problems have come together. In one chapter, prisoners with drug problems are greatly helped by working with animals. Statistics show that 64 percent of ex-convicts return to jail, while inmates who worked with animals during their incarceration had a recidivism rate of just 16 percent.

Many of the animals in this book have been rescued from terrible places, and both the animals and the people who took them in got a second chance to have a good life.

INTRODUCTION

THIS BOOK IS about people trying to heal the damage done to animals and how animals heal suffering human beings. Some people do it one animal at a time, making room in their urban backyards, basements, and bedrooms. Others have carved out refuges for creatures in shopping malls, nursing homes, and even jails. Still others help by trying to pass legislation that would hold breeders accountable, require wide-scale spaying and neutering, ban dogfighting, and prevent horses from being shipped to slaughter.

The stories are about the animals who sit in their laps, lick their hands, and sleep in their beds, who return from abuse and starvation to some degree of health and trust, who repay immeasurably the favors done to them. Because what rescued animals do best and most astonishingly is forgive. They may or may not forget what was done to them—how could they?—but they invariably forgive. Somewhere between memory and expectation (as author and horsewoman Jane Smiley characterizes animal and human relationships), they manage to revive their trust in and love for humans, even though certain people have hurt them grievously.

Ours is a reciprocal relationship: we need creatures and the qualities they show us and elicit in us. The human and animal bond keeps us alive in places within ourselves that would wither without love, without humor, without complete and constant acceptance.

This human need for affection and connection does not stop when someone can afford to buy everything—except human love, as we see with Bob Bradley, a wealthy polo player with a broken heart who is attended to by his pal Jack, a devoted herding dog. And neither does it stop when the person is poor, a fact well known by Christine Madruga, who runs a California pet rescue group. She helped provide a kennel for dogs owned by homeless people living in the desert so that the pets as well as their owners can have shelter. The need does not stop when it comes to people who are mentally ill or handicapped, as Lori Sarner discovered when she began bringing unwanted and injured horses together with damaged children and adults at the Pegasus Riding Academy for the Handicapped.

If media coverage, animal activism, changes in animal protection statutes, and the growth of vegetarianism are any indication, the world is raising its collective awareness of the need for kindness to our fellow creatures. At no time in history has there been such a critical mass of people working to improve conditions for companion animals, for wild animals, and for farm animals. *Growth hormone free, not tested on animals, free range,* and *organic* have become premium labels on food and products for people and for pets. Even McDonald's has bowed to pressure and now requires improved conditions for the chickens raised by its suppliers. In the words of Susan Heywood, fund-raiser extraordinaire for the Scratch & Sniff Foundation, an animal welfare group based in Phoenix, Arizona, we seem to be more aware "that we are responsible for what we have tamed."

Photographer Judy Olausen and I are longtime friends and colleagues and lifelong animal lovers. When we decided to explore this relationship between humans and animals, we found that the problem wasn't finding examples; the problem was limiting the number of them—there are so many stories, and they are literally everywhere. Friends, strangers, neighbors, family, coworkers—everyone has a powerful animal story to tell if you just ask.

The love of animals and the need for what they give us is like a common language we share regardless of our age, class, gender, race, education, or political persuasion.

I often walk up to people and start asking them about their critter. At a steeplechase near Middleburg, Virginia, for example, I was enjoying the horse scene, when I saw a dear little sheltie and a nicely dressed gentleman leading her. I stooped down to pet the dog, and the man and I began talking. He told me how humane officers had rescued her from a basement, nearly dead from starvation, how he could empathize because of his childhood abuse, and how he loved this dog. He referred me to Bob and Patricia Reever, the couple that subsequently cared for the dog and placed her with him, and they are profiled in this book.

Judy and I share a similar passion for animals, which allowed our subjects to talk freely with us. In fact, they did much more than talk—they fed us, welcomed us into their homes and farms, and showed us their photographs. They drove us around and took us with them to shelters. Our keen interest got us invited into their lives, and they trusted us to document their stories. It got us into a jail, a hospice, nursing homes, a polo club, the most dangerous ghetto in the country, a private board meeting, and behind the scenes at more than one riding facility for the handicapped.

This collection represents just a fraction of the stories we sifted from the possible multitude. Americans today own an unprecedented number of pets: an estimated sixty-three million dogs and seventy-three million cats. At the same time, humane societies receive more than six to eight million unwanted animals each year and euthanize three to four million unwanted cats and dogs annually. More than forty thousand horses from the United States go to slaughter in Mexican plants every year and thousands more in Canadian processing plants. In addition, twenty thousand greyhounds are disposed of after every racing season—they are shot, injected, gassed, thrown live to the alligators in Florida canals, or burned in mounds, their tattooed ears cut off so they cannot be identified.

Movies and advertising campaigns unintentionally spawn more tragedy. The children's animated film *101 Dalmatians* prompted thousands of parents to buy Dalmatian puppies, which do not make good pets for children. The Taco Bell commercial featuring a digitally-altered talking Chihuahua brought thousands of tiny dogs into homes where they were not properly cared for. Crazes for potbellied pigs, emus and ostriches, llamas, and donkeys have resulted in similar increases in animal casualties. By any standard, this degree of suffering and these staggering death rates constitute an animal catastrophe. It is inexcusable. It is unnecessary. And it is preventable. What we hope to address with *Saved* is that these precious beings deserve better.

When we mistreat animals, we miss out on what they have to teach us: forgiveness, compassion, and unconditional love. This is what Hilleary Bogley tries to instill in the children she meets in the Virginia hills, where dogs spend their lives starving on short, heavy chains. She may bring dog food (as well as food for their owners), but what she hopes to nourish is the same empathetic understanding and great-hearted-ness in people that dogs—even abused dogs—have in abundance.

As Judy and I traveled from coast to coast, we visited people who care for animals one on one and others who are organized on a formidable and effective scale to raise money and awareness. We also saw forgiveness extended to people over and over again: by horses that had been beaten, dogs that had been tortured, cats turned out to fend for themselves, and ferrets left to starve in a cage in an empty apartment. They forgive not by religious dogma or moral principle, but because they love without thought or reservation. They trust again in circumstances where perhaps a human being would remember the abuse and never regain trust. In St. Louis, Missouri, we met Quentin, a dog that made the ultimate leap of forgiveness—he survived the animal pound gas chamber and lived to love and work with Randy Grim, rescuing dogs from the streets on behalf of Stray Rescue St. Louis.

These animals are only asking for a chance, some kind words, and food and shelter, and when they receive them—through the generosity of, say, Patricia Reever, who takes the most damaged, medically expensive, and ill animals into her home in Fairfax, Virginia—their voiceless gratitude is boundless.

The animals we met found a friend in their rescuers—and that friendship worked both ways. As a wheelchair-bound woman in an Arizona nursing home said simply about a little mongrel who visits her: "I have a lot of depression, and he helps me."

Much of the abuse and neglect is related to pet overpopulation. We cannot adopt our way out of this crisis, which is powered by short gestation periods and abundant fertility. Prevention, through rigorous spay and neuter programs—subsidized for those who cannot afford the cost—is essential. Not doing what is necessary to resolve this crisis cannot be justified as a matter of economics. It would actually cost less to prevent the births of unwanted animals than to rescue, shelter, euthanize, and dispose of them.

Never before in human history has more money been allocated to animals: in food, gourmet treats, fancy beds and carriers, doggie day care, luxurious stables, animal chiropractors, acupuncturists, and psychologists, and pet grooming services. Companion animal care is a multibillion dollar business. Yet the plight of the millions of mistreated animals remains hidden. We have an obligation to care for animals, to consider their highest welfare, to treat each creature with compassion, and to never—ever—put them in a position where we will need their forgiveness.

SAVED

The dogs play with Kim Evans, a resident of the home who suffers from cerebral palsy.

MY WHITE ANGELS

DON AND DARLENE AHLSTROM AND THEIR DOGS, CHANCE AND
HOPE, AT L'AMOUR ET L'ABRI HOSPICE AND ADULT FOSTER CARE

KIM EVANS'S EYELASHES are long and thick as a pony's, and she
looks through them with large dark-blue eyes, her head cocked perma-
nently sideways against the black leather neck support. Beyond the cuffs of
her plaid shirt, her nails sport cherry-colored polish on hands bent double
against their wrists. Kim is tiny—about half the weight of each of the two
great white dogs that gaze at her, lick her hands, and bump softly against
her immaculate white tennis shoes as she sits lashed to the blue wheelchair.

Chance, the male, and Hope, the female, are Great Pyrenees herding
dogs with low-slung tails and wet, kind brown eyes set in drifts of snowy
hair. When they move away from Kim—through the two living rooms of
the large rambler to Michelle's bed or Peter's chair or to visit Mildred in the
recliner—they make a scuffing noise on the gray carpet, each one hopping
on three legs.

Out beyond the deck and past the horse barn, long slim v's of geese are
gliding down into the snowy corn stubble in the late winter fields around
Rochester, Minnesota.

Don and Darlene Ahlstrom opened this small suburban hospice and adult foster care, L'amour et L'abri (love and labor), in 1984 and named it in honor of the years they'd spent in France while Don was in the Air Force.

In 1998, the couple saw a television news show featuring the dogs, which had been found in a ditch, starving and crippled. The Wright County Humane Society was making a plea for medical funds for Chance and Hope, who hobbled hopefully toward the cameraman, each dragging a useless hind leg. The society received seventeen thousand dollars in donations—enough to pay for surgery to amputate the legs and to start a fund for other abandoned, abused animals in need of surgery. Hundreds of people applied to the society to adopt the dogs. Don and Darlene, the last to be interviewed, won custody.

Chance and Hope are now canine caretakers for the residents at the home, which serves as hospice and as long-term permanent care for five severely disabled people.

"I work for God," says Darlene. "These are beings I can love and care for, where I feel like I can do some good. This is the home of love and spoil."

The oldest resident, Mildred, in her late eighties, has Alzheimer's disease. "I have been here five weeks," she declares, over the sound of *Animal Planet* on the TV, her right hand stroking Chance, who often lies next to her recliner. "She has been here four years," Darlene whispers.

Michelle, resting in a mobile bed with an IV looping away from her arm, has end-stage multiple sclerosis. She once worked in an animal shelter and loves horses as well as dogs and cats. She can no longer move, but her eyes follow the dogs around the room.

Peter, in a wheelchair similar to Kim's, has severe cerebral palsy. He has been here eighteen years and looks half his age—a boyish forty. He is less in control of his body than Kim and seems less aware of contact, although Darlene speaks to him just as she does to anyone else.

"There are lots of angels here, and Darlene's one of them," says Peter's mother, Carol. Darlene, in turn, calls Chance and Hope "my white angels." The angels rise early and hop from bedroom to bedroom, taking inventory, greeting each person. Their enormous tails sweep slowly like great white plumes behind them.

The angels also have idiosyncrasies. "Every weekday at 12:38 p.m., they howl at *The Bold and the Beautiful* theme," says Darlene. "We don't know why. It's the only one they do that with."

Darlene limps too, the toll from keeping up a house with three kitchens, half a dozen bedrooms, meeting rooms, and recreation rooms, and raising four children and two of her eleven grandchildren.

Wheelchair ramps for the residents make it easier for Chance and Hope to hop down to the garden, where a pergola provides shade above a fountain and a collection of bird feeders donated by Poppa, a former resident who died at age ninety-five.

"We got the dogs five weeks after their surgeries, and they could hardly make it outside and down the ramp to go potty," Darlene explains. The University of Minnesota veterinarian who treated Chance and Hope estimated the dogs were about ten months old when they were struck by a forceful swing with a bat or iron bar. When discovered in the ditch, they were between a year and a half and two years old.

"For having been beaten, they do trust. I hope they forgot. I hope they don't dream about it," says Darlene.

Chance and Hope seem to know something about having sound minds and good hearts trapped inside injured bodies.

Kim, in her mid-twenties, will be here for life. When she laughs—fragmented, wet cries—she raises her arms, her elbows half-bent like wings. The dogs snuffle at her to make her giggle. At lunch, Darlene cradles Kim's head and spoons minced chicken and rice into her mouth or holds a glass of milk to her lips, a white towel tucked under Kim's chin to catch saliva. Chance dozes under the trestle table. "Good girl," says Darlene. Kim gurgles.

Chance and Hope check each patient at bedtime, hopping softly from room to room—to Michelle's room, where a photo of a big bay Budweiser Clydesdale looms over a laughing Michelle. The photo holds the place of honor among stuffed plush horses, horse pillows, stuffed unicorn toys, and a horse-collar clock.

The dogs move cheerfully on to Kim's room, where a small ornamental china plaque declares, "It's Hard Being a Princess," and wild horses gallop on the wallpaper border above a single hospital bed draped in a white chenille coverlet. On the shelf is a treasured photo of Kim's boyfriend, Randy, who also has cerebral palsy.

Chance and Hope, jesters, comforters, guardians in the night, also sit nearby when residents die. "The dogs are there then, and they are very quiet," says Darlene, her hands deep in their fine, clean fur.

"Do you believe in angels?" she asks. "I do. I have them here all the time."

SHE'S MY GIRL

WALT AND BEVERLY KUCHLER AND THEIR DONKEYS AND HORSES

THE DONKEYS COME trotting in pairs when Walt Kuchler calls them: Abigail and Patches, Sunshine and Snowflake, Pancho and Dusty. They are bushy browed and pixie hooved, with dorsal stripes running from their outsized ears to their undersized tails atop bodies that are cream and pinto and gray.

And then there is Mabel. Mabel is a bay Percheron mix with a black mane so thick it cascades down both sides of her huge neck. A nine-year-old mare with the sloe eyes of a belly dancer that belie her sixteen-hundred-pound physique, she is darkly feminine and built like a medieval war horse.

"She got a butt on her," says Walt admiringly, brushing the big mare. "It was love at first sight. I love big drafts. She's my girl. I couldn't sell her for a hundred grand; I like her that much. People up here got their champion bred this, outta a champion that, and I'm just as proud of Mabel. I love you, girl."

Walt is 6½ feet tall, leggy, wearing a tan cowboy hat decorated with a horsehair hat band, and so tanned by the high mountain sun that "People think I'm a Mexican," he says with a wide flash of very white teeth beneath a salt-and-pepper mustache.

He and his wife, Beverly, and their herd live in the Garner Valley of California, a community of thirteen hundred in meadows thick with Ponderosa and Jeffries pines flanked by the San Jacinto Mountains. On the morning we arrived, up the hairpin turns from the desert 4650 feet below, the valley looked eerily familiar, and it was: scenes from the 1960s TV series *Bonanza* and *The Cisco Kid* were filmed in this valley, and car commercials are filmed here today. Walt and Bev's yellow geodesic dome home sits in a grove of pines on a small rise.

"This house was a repo, total trash, and it stunk so bad you couldn't be in it for more 'n five minutes," says Walt, who spent months hauling trash to the dump. They share the house with an African Grey parrot, three dogs, five fish, and a gecko. The house overlooks the pole barn and paddock that Mabel occupies with a sorrel quarter horse named Tex. The sign at the front gate reads: Camp Kuchler. "Everybody up here's got a ranch or a hacienda, so I'm campin' with my horses," Walt explains.

In 2000, Bev and Walt and their son, Sam, were living in Orange County. Bev worked for the phone company; Walt was a pipe fitter. Sam was tall like his dad and trim with blue eyes. He played high-school football and was goalie for every water polo game at his school, Valencia High.

"Kids are cool—I loved being a dad," says Walt. "I didn't babysit my kid; I raised him. I always hugged on him. But when he turned thirteen, I hugged him and he said, 'Dad, what are you, gay?' I said it's a man hug; there's nothing wrong with a guy hugging his son or his dad."

"He called me Belly Boy," says Walt, patting a modest middle-aged paunch. "It was his way of screwing with me. That's the handle on my CB in my jeep. He called me Wally too. That's a kid's way of saying they love you."

Then Sam went to college. "He hung around with the wrong guys, drank beer with them, and they kept bugging him to try heroin," says Walt. "One night, his resistance was low. That's all it took."

Walter Kuchler rides Mabel, his rescued draft-horse cross, on the mountain trails of California.

Sam entered chemical rehabilitation treatment twice. "It's pretty sad when you go into rehab and listen to your son talk about putting a needle in his arm and crying in the bathroom. When you're the parent, you are supposed to protect him," Walt says.

At twenty, Sam and his girlfriend placed their newborn son into a sealed adoption. Ten months later, Sam died of a heroin overdose, sitting on a toilet with a needle in his arm. "They didn't know if they should get married or keep it or what," Walt explains. "He was asking me, 'Dad, what do I do?' I said it's up to you. So he adopted his baby out. It's a closed adoption through the Mormons, and now Sam is gone and we can't find the baby, and that sucks. I wish I had my grandson."

Bev and Walt quit their jobs and fled Orange County for the mountains, acquiring the donkeys and horses along the way. Now Walt visits drug rehabilitation facilities, doing what he can to prevent tragedy for other families.

"I take a picture of Sam hugging his mom, and I take his ashes in the urn and a picture of him dead on the toilet of the heroin overdose," he says. "I hand 'em to the kids and freak 'em out. They are good kids, but kids do some stupid stuff. I just tell 'em my story. And I say go home and hug your parents; they love you more than anything. If you die they will cry every day."

"There's a war going on in this country, but this one they don't put in the paper," Walt adds. "There are kids dying and the obituaries aren't telling the truth, why they are dying. Before my kid was on drugs, I thought addicts were scumbags—when I went to rehabs, I saw they are just ordinary, normal people. It's in every family. President Bush had a drinking problem, his daughter has a drinking problem—it's everywhere."

Now Bev makes quilts at home, and Walt and Mabel ride the mountain trails. "I can't get enough riding; I ride anytime if anyone wants to go," says Walt, saddling Mabel as ravens call in the pines among the boulders. He fits her with a leather breast collar, an outsized western saddle, and a bridle with a copper mouth roller bit. Mabel spins the roller with her tongue, champing, and makes a muted rattle.

"I ride with women," he says. "The guys don't ride much here. I like to go for five or six hours, and I call the guys' horses rental horses 'cause they only ride for one hour. I just take a bunch of aspirin and go."

He purchased Mabel from a ranch in Anza despite the fact that she was, says Walt, "all messed up—the shoer hit her in the face with a file. I couldn't even sit on her she was so wild."

That was lucky for Mabel, since unrideable horses, especially big fleshy ones like Mabel, often go to the horse-meat or "killer" buyers. It took a good two years of loving and being nice to that horse, says Walt, before he was riding her and she began to trust him.

"Then one day we were ridin' and my hat blew off, and she took off. I lost a stirrup and reins, she ran for the low trees, and I went to the hospital. I was on crutches, black and blue from my hip to my ankle. I was within inches of selling her."

It took another year, but Walt rode again. "Although we were both shaking when I got on," he concedes. He just had to ride, he says.

"My heart's broke. When your kid dies—parents who lose a kid know—you wanna die and be with your kid. And when you're riding a horse, you have to think about it, have to pay attention. You become one with the animal. Like they say: the outside of a horse is good for the inside of a man. When you ride, all your hurts and problems go away."

"Is there something wrong with me 'cause I kiss my horses?" he asks unabashedly. "And I hug 'em every night. When I go out and feed, I hug every one of them. I love havin' my critters. I wish Sam could be here; he loved dogs . . ."

Walt has an idea that what heals him would help others, particularly addicts. "First off, it doesn't do good to put people in jail for drugs," he says. "You put 'em in an environment with animals, put 'em in the woods, have 'em do some work, get away from the city, and do that for a year or two. People are nicer out in the country. The city is all blacktop and buildings. *This* is where God's at."

Sunshine, the saucy gray donkey filly, attempts to climb into the golf

Walt's only child died of a heroin overdose, and riding Mabel brings him peace. "Out here is where God is at," he says. "When you ride, all your hurts and problems go away."

cart Walt and Bev use to drive between the donkey pasture and the house. "The donkeys are sweet," says Bev. "If I have fresh lipstick on when I go out to see them, by the time I get done they have pink stuff on their faces."

"The animals help, because it's holding onto them and loving them that brings peace," says Bev. "These are our babies, and we love them like our family. Walter's always saying I'd bring them in the house if I could."

"Animals are it; they take your heartache away," said Walt. "I lost my boy to drugs, and my horse saved my life—just the therapy of riding. Animals are God's gift to us."

3

SOLID LOVE

LYNNE WARFEL-HOLT AND HER DOGS AND HORSES

SATURDAY MORNING WAS special when Lynne Warfel-Holt was a child. That was the morning she would awaken early to watch *The Cisco Kid* and other TV cowboy shows. "I'd sit on the arm of a chair with a pillow for a saddle and string reins, and I rode," she remembers. "Or I'd pretend to be a horse, and make Mom put a pan of water on the floor for me to drink."

"Animals were part of who I was, but I didn't have any," says Lynne, who was an only child. "When I was three, Mom found me trying to make a pet of a big furry spider behind the kitchen range. In Hershey Park they found me sitting with a chained raccoon in my lap. I always felt better with animals."

As soon as she could write, she learned to fill out entry forms and mail them in to win-a-horse contests. "Like Ovaltine, where you could win a Shetland pony with a bridle and saddle. Each time I thought, 'God is going to let me win!' And at every birthday and every Christmas, they'd ask me, 'What do you want?' and I'd say, 'I want a horse!'"

When she was seven, her family moved to a farm in Pennsylvania. "I thought for sure now they were gonna get me a horse—they got a divorce instead," she says.

In 1957, Lynne watched Walt Disney's *Miracle of the White Stallions* three times straight through, weeping, especially when the Lipizzan stallions of the Spanish Riding School trot single file across the ring to Schubert's March Militaire. "Please don't let me go back to the real world; here's where I want to be," Lynne thought.

It was decades later—when she was forty-three—that a rescued horse named Twister gave her access to that world. He was a young Arabian-Thoroughbred cross, and Lynne purchased him for seven hundred dollars from a Minnesota animal shelter that had rescued him from starvation.

"A horse trainer who went with me to the shelter to look at him told me his neck looked like it was on backwards and he was back at the knee. And he had big ears and looked like a half-grown mule—not an attractive specimen," Lynne says. "But he was so calm and sweet—he has the biggest heart and licks you like a golden retriever—that I decided to take him home."

On a December day, knowing Twister was being delivered to her boarding barn, Lynne felt like that hopeful little girl she had been every Christmas Eve growing up. "When he arrived, I bawled like a baby. I was so happy," says Lynne. "Outside of when my children were born, it was the happiest I'd been in my life."

Lynne graduated from seminary intending to become a Presbyterian pastor, but she ended up acting in movies and on radio and stage. Her family includes her British musician husband, two sons, an African Grey parrot, assorted dogs, cats, and guinea pigs, and, for the moment, four horses.

"I've made some bad choices in love relationships; I had all this love nobody seemed to want except my animals," she says. "People could say about my having a lot of horses and dogs: 'Oh, she's another damn bleeding heart or psychologically dysfunctional person with problems she transfers to animals,' but it is not like that. Animals teach me everything about love, and especially they teach forgiveness and grace."

She found Francis, a basset hound puppy, when she began volunteering in rescue for springer spaniels and Gordon setters and helping a friend care for animals from a local puppy mill. The puppy, originally a pet-store purchase, had been through eight foster homes in thirteen weeks.

Francis's last home did not allow dogs, "So the woman hid him in her basement," says Lynne. "She cut his food down so he wouldn't poop. He weighed about as much as a cat and looked like a skeleton with a head. He could hardly hold his head up; he was so skinny, and he fell on his ears. He would growl and snap if you tried to pick him up when he was lying down or napping on the sofa. He was fearful he was going back into a kennel alone in a basement."

"It took him a long while to trust that he was really staying in this wonderful place," she says. "Now he is one of the most gregarious, cuddly dogs I have ever owned. He is happiness personified and makes me laugh every day—especially when he goofs around with my massive male Gordon setter, Pumbaa, who is also a hugging fool."

"Some people say animals can't answer, can't communicate with us; the hell they can't!" Lynne insists. "Animals are the only beings that understand me. I can look them in the eye and it's like, gotcha? Gotcha! They look at you, and it really is a sentient being saying, 'I'm so grateful you love me, and I have this life now. God bless you and thank you for helping me.' Same thing for me. I look at them and I tell them, 'God bless you because to you I'm not nuts; there is a being that can take what I am.'"

"People always scared me," confesses Lynne. "I'm a real shy person. Because I have a good speaking voice, I seem sure of myself, but actually I am a scared kid on the inside. The animals say, 'Hey, little girl, you don't have to be scared.' They love me. I don't have to worry about did I say the right thing, the wrong thing, do they agree with my politics? Am I funny or pretty or too fat?"

While seminary was intellectually exciting, Lynne says there was much she didn't learn at seminary spiritually. Animals have mended that gap. "They teach me everything there is to know about what God is: love, graciousness, and forgiveness."

"My horse Twister is a hundred percent solid love," she says. "He tries so hard always to do whatever you teach him. He gives huge wet licks if you put your hand out, or he'll put his nose in your face, never once nipping or biting. He would never be bad-tempered about anything. He's my seven-hundred-dollar wonder horse. When he's lying in the field, I can go out and lie on top of him in the sun and nap along with him. He's the horse I'll never let go. He's my friend."

Lynne's most prized possession is an autographed photo of famed primate anthropologist Jane Goodall, with the words, "For Lynne, just hear your heart." Lynne's heart is full of animals.

"I was taught only humans go to heaven, and Rene Descartes said animals are just machines. I got distressed about this until my cousin said, 'Haven't you read Genesis 9? "I will create a covenant between you and me and all living creatures on the earth." God won't have a heaven where not everything we love is there. God says how much he loves creatures. And Job12: "Ask the beasts and they shall teach thee."'"

Showing concern for animals is a matter of taking the side of the weak against the strong, something the best people have always done, Lynne says, citing Mohandas Gandhi: "The greatness of a nation and its moral progress can be judged by the way its animal are treated."

Today one of Lynne's four horses is a Lipizzan, the son of a white stallion from the Spanish Riding School in Vienna, and although Lynne hasn't yet trotted down the center line to music wearing a shadbelly coat and a top hat, she creates music for riders who perform the ancient art of dressage as practiced to perfection in the movie she saw long ago.

"Dogs give me laughter, and horses give me art, and they all give me love. I am so eternally grateful," says Lynne. "Everything I wanted when I was four, I have it now."

4

BROUGHT INTO BRIGHTNESS

BEVERLY AND DON MCCORMACK, ANDREA MCCORMACK,
AND THEIR DOGS

WHEN A POLICE officer in this lakeside village in Minnesota picked up a stray dog, he always knew where it would find shelter. He would call Beverly and Don McCormack, whose fenced yard was home to the springer spaniels Beverly bred and to many lost dogs as well.

"He'd call and ask, 'Bev, have you got room for another dog?' And she'd take it, run an ad, and many times we'd get a call from the owners," says Don. "For twenty years, our home served as the town's unofficial dog pound."

If Bev and Don provided safety for the lost dogs of White Bear Lake, Minnesota, the dogs provided Don and Bev and their four children with consolation, connection, and delight.

Andrea, their oldest child, met her husband, Rich, when they were walking their respective dogs. The dogs—a collie named Siri and a Brittany spaniel named Lucy—were part of their wedding ceremony in a Wisconsin park. "Dogs have been important to each of us," says Andrea, an artist. "There have been a lot of tragedies throughout the family, and dogs are a stabilizing force for us."

Beverly McCormack suffers from dementia but still responds to Duke, the cheerful best buddy of her husband, Don.

Andrea was severely scalded when she was three and spent six months undergoing skin grafts. Don's and Beverly's mothers both died in tragic ways. And Andrea's brother was convicted and imprisoned for a crime so dark the family will not speak about it.

A constant in her adult life, a collie goes everywhere with Andrea. Her first was Lucy (the name means light in Latin), and Siri, the current one, is Norwegian for beauty and victory, she says. "Despite the personal trials and tragedies we experienced, the dogs always provided a source of joy and love," says Andrea. "They showed us that was available to us in the world."

"Lucy was like a Zen dog—she taught me to be in the moment, the quality of what love is, the everlasting and ephemeral nature of it," says Andrea. "Now I am always more conscious of the attention I give to Siri. Dogs live for less time than we do, and in that short time, it's important to love completely."

In 1997, Beverly was diagnosed with frontal lobe dementia, a degenerative neurological condition. It was rapid and devastating. Her biggest concern when the family sought a nursing home for her was that she could be near a dog. For six years, before dementia made her incontinent and incoherent, she lived in a nursing home with two dogs and a cat.

Don, a retired postal worker and insurance agent, lived alone, missing Bev and their animals. Then his neighbor went to the dog pound, he explains, to adopt a cat. She found herself a cat and found something else for Don. "There was an eight-month-old puppy there that she liked," says Don. "'Well, say good-bye,' they told her, 'because tomorrow he goes—his five days here are up.' She couldn't stand that, so she bought him, too, and she gave him to us."

Duke is a German shepherd mix with a golden wolf-like coat and honey-colored eyes; the tips of his ears fold downward, and he greets everyone with a half grin, half pant, his gently curled tail wagging.

Andrea, Don, and Duke visit Bev these days at the Alterra Memory Enhancement Center, a nursing home in North Oaks, Minnesota. The façade of dementia care there is cheery: the hallway to Bev's room consists of Victorian-style shop fronts, rocking chairs beckon on miniature veran-dahs, gas fires crackle on sitting-room hearths. The walls are hung with black-and-white photos of Charlie Chaplin, Lauren Bacall, George Burns, and other stars of a gentler century. Through the windows are views of bird feeders and wind chimes.

Don, in his eighties, is trim and neatly dressed in a denim shirt, pressed khakis, sneakers, and a baseball cap. Duke and Don pass across the cobble-stone floor of the lobby. A young woman shouts, "Breathe! In and out. In and out!" to seniors sitting in a circle and then leads them in "Row, row, row your boat." Some join in, others sit and stare. In the background, like a distant bird, a frail voice cries, "Help, help, help!"

"Should I put him on the schedule?" asks Maureen, a staffer whose name tag identifies her as a life enrichment coordinator. "When we do exercise and Duke comes in, they all stop. They'd rather see the dog."

Bev is in her seventies, slight and soft with fine-skinned pink cheeks and large eyes. Her jaws work constantly, while her eyes move from Don to Duke to Andrea to us and back to Duke. The only sounds she makes are faint groans and an occasional breathy "yeeaaaahhh," more air than conso-nants. Duke pokes his nose across the coverlet close to her cheek, with an intent, happy, willing look on his face. Bev's eyes roll toward him, fix on him.

"They keep those rolls of cloth in her hands because she digs at her hand," Don explains. "And the first time she saw Duke here, she stopped digging at them and put her hand out and smiled."

Now that Bev's memories are darkened and tangled by her disease, Duke provides sunlight. "I'm not sure she recognizes me," says Don, "but she rec-ognizes him!"

Two young, sturdy women wearing back supports lift Bev from the bed to a wheelchair; there is the rustle of diapers as they adjust her. The assistants smooth her flowered red dress and white cardigan and belt her upright into the chair. She is rolled through the home—to meals, to a window—Duke's toenails clicking on the tiles as he walks alongside her chair.

"The perverse blessing of my mother's illness is that she has lost memory of the bad things," Andrea says.

Now, at home, Duke goes everywhere with Don—chews his shoes, tips over the waste baskets, follows him from room to room, waits outside the bathroom, rides in the car on errands. Recently, Don found lumps under Duke's chin: diagnosed with a fast-moving lymphoma, Duke has been undergoing chemotherapy and radiation. He has eleven treatments to go and is in remission at the moment. "He's only five; he's too vital and vibrant and intelligent not to try and save him," says Don. Then he concedes, "Treatment is probably as much for me as for him."

"He gives me a way to fill a need—he has to eat, go outside—he makes me responsible," says Don. "He's more buddy than he is dog."

5

UNDERCOVER PARTNERS

CARRIE AND HER DOG, GRISSOM; RICK AND HIS DOG, ALLY

WHEN CARRIE AND Rick are working, their youth, their size, and their cute pets present an unassuming, friendly picture: girl and boy walking dogs. Grissom, Carrie's dog, is a muscular liver-and-white mix of springer spaniel and Labrador with a dash of terrier, while Rick's dog, Ally, is a petite gold mongrel.

In reality, Carrie and Rick are undercover deputies in a county drug enforcement division—"narcs"—and Grissom and Ally are canine detectives—"dope dogs." "Seek dope!" is the command. When Carrie and Rick give it, their two small dogs seem electrified. Tails wagging, they scamper nose to the ground in zigzags or leap onto shelves or dig at piles of rubbish.

Dogs that detect drugs are trained to sit when they find what they are looking for. When Grissom sits, he thinks he has found his squeaky baseball toy, a reward that Carrie keeps in her fanny pack.

Behind the smoked windows of her SUV, Carrie takes a break, her forty-caliber Walther tucked in with her Mountain Dew between the front seats, Grissom chewing his squeaky toy in a kennel in the back.

Drug-sniffing dogs Grissom and Ally are more than business partners with Minneapolis narcotics department detectives Carrie and Rick—they are beloved members of the family.

"It's a lotta long hours and the most dangerous people," Carrie says. "Dealers have absolutely nothing to lose." It's also sometimes frustrating—not for Grissom, who always gets his satisfying treat—but for the officers. "The government spends a lot of court time and effort and doesn't get a lot out of it," Carrie explains. "We see dealers go to court and get second and third and fourth chances."

Grissom got his own last chance when a narcotics detection dog trainer visited a suburban animal shelter seeking a replacement trainee for a retiring dog. The trainer was searching among the throwaway dogs for the right personality. Grissom had already been adopted out and returned to the shelter numerous times, bombing out of the job of being a good companion animal. He had too much energy for people who had insufficient time to work with him, and he also had a sort of canine attention deficit disorder.

"He had very bad manners," says Carrie. "He was a mess. He was unruly. He still doesn't like to sit. Now he loves his job; he would work until he died."

Grissom has ridden with Carrie at a hundred miles per hour pursuing drug dealers down back roads. And he sleeps next to her bed. In between, he mostly uses his hunting skills and extraordinary nose to search for drugs and drug-scented money. "Last month," says Carrie, consulting her log, "we found around twenty-seven thousand dollars in cash, three hundred grams of marijuana, and fifteen ounces of crack."

Carrie, who earned a child psychology degree prior to becoming an undercover officer, likes her job despite the hours, the danger, and the contact with people with what she calls "simple thought processes and immature temperaments."

"It's fun to solve mysteries, to evolve and work through a challenge, to be creative and get somebody," she says.

To Carrie and Rick, it's work, albeit enjoyable work. To Grissom and Ally, it's play. Grissom is an optimist; it's easy to see in his happy grin and his confident, bouncy walk. Even tucked in his kennel in the rear compartment of her SUV, he seems to smile, and he listens keenly, gnawing a rubber toy, his yellow eyes on Carrie's face.

Recently, the optimistic rookie got his U.S. Police Canine Association certification—graduation day for Grissom. To earn it, he passed a field test, finding two drug stashes among five cars, and two drug stashes in three rooms. That degree hung on the close-knit communication between Grissom and Carrie.

"A lot of testing is about me, my behavior and handling skills," she says. "Ninety percent of the time if he does it wrong, it will be my fault, anything from not putting him on the scent cone to not pointing to the right things for him to look at. Grissom is mellowing out, taking more time and getting more detailed on his own. At first, he would go through the rooms at two hundred miles an hour, so hyper and excited. Now he knows nobody will make him leave until he is done, and there will be another day."

Carrie grew up in an apartment with a single mother and was "deathly allergic to all animals," she says, but she yearned to have a dog. "I just love them, and now I love being Grissom's buddy," she says. "Steve, the police dog trainer, kept telling me he's goofy-looking and weird and mangy. I think he's just so cute! I love him and wouldn't know what to do without him."

In addition to police work, Grissom has developed a repertoire of pet tricks: he can sit, stay, lie down, and shake, and he's mastering roll over. Carrie, who is partner, parent, and friend to Grissom, says, "I'm so very attached. I drop him off tonight at the kennels for the first time, because my husband and I are going out of town, and I know it's harder on me than on him."

Grissom, the reject, the failure, has become Grissom the glowing success. "A lot of animals could be brilliant, wonderful pets and have talents to offer," Carrie says of her last-chance dog. "They never get a chance."

Ally, who also got her opportunity through the police force, is a worrier and a dog with a painful wish to please. Barely larger than a fox, with a white muzzle and grave, brown eyes, she is perhaps a blend of yellow Labrador and corgie. Unlike the confident Grissom, Ally cringes in her kennel when strangers address her—the legacy of abuse. "She was beat real bad," says Rick. "When I leave her alone, she tucks her tail at people. She is afraid of pillows and couch cushions. Someone really scared her."

Rick had been an undercover officer for two years when Ally became his partner and moved in with him. It was, he admits, mutually beneficial. "It was a once-in-a-lifetime opportunity," he says. "I was single, living in a townhouse, going out all the time. She definitely brought me more responsibility, and I needed it. Working in narcotics is a lotta fun, a really good job, and being a narc with a dog is the best of both worlds to me."

Ally thinks so too, apparently. "When she finds dope and gets her toy, she is very proud of herself—she prances around with her chest out," Rick says. "She's a little hero."

And work she does. All told, Ally has found twelve million dollars' worth of drugs—methamphetamine, cocaine, crack, heroin, tar heroin, mushrooms, ecstasy, hashish, and marijuana. Twice she found seventeen pounds of meth in the bumper of a car, and once she nosed out ninety thousand dollars of drug money in a bag in a closet. She is a sort of summa cum laude of canine drug detectives, and she ranked second in the United States for indoors search at the Police Canine Association trials.

"Narc dogs have to have good play drive," Rick explains. "Ally thinks she's finding her tennis ball. And they have excellent concentration: Ally would rather take her toy than have food. She is completely focused and will look for hours; I am not kidding."

In this game of hide-and-seek, the risks to officers and dogs are guns and drugs and addicts using both. "We work crack houses, where usually six or more people are sitting around and selling and smoking," Rick explains. "It's guaranteed to have guns."

While narcotics officers ordinarily do not take their dogs into a site until the suspects have been removed, there are other perils. Some sites have mouse poison. Sometimes the menace turns out to be more tennis balls that distract the dogs from the hunt because they are seen as a reward. And some houses are so filthy, Rick says, "I ain't gonna put my dog in there."

At other times, Rick and Ally focus on upper-level dealers, whom Rick describes as "clean-cut, bigger people who look more responsible because it's a business; it's very big money."

"People would be amazed at what kind of problem it is," says Rick. "The dealers are so crafty in how they hide stuff that without the dogs we wouldn't find it. Ally found kilos wrapped in twenty-one layers of axle grease, dryer sheets, plastic bags, coffee grounds, and other things to mask the scent. People are making heroin liquid, soaking blankets in it, and then drying them. If the dog hits on a pile of blankets, and you can't find anything, there's no way you would be able to figure it out. That's where a dog is great."

Rick spends his ten- to twelve-hour workdays escorted by Ally. When he's in the narcotics squad office, Ally moves from desk to desk for pats, and she will jump up on an officer's desk, lie down on the paperwork, and demand to have her belly scratched. "My wife wants me out of this job like now; she's had enough," says Rick. "I will stay until they let me retire and keep Ally."

In his rare leisure time, Rick says, "I can lie down and hug a dog—Ally—for hours. The worst thing about this job is the hours. The best thing is the dog."

6

MARICOPA MASH

SHERIFF JOE ARPAIO AND THE MARICOPA COUNTY
SHERIFF'S OFFICE ANIMAL SAFE HOSPICE

THE TOUGHEST SHERIFF in the country, the guy who stalked drug runners in the mountains of Turkey and in Mexico City, who capped his thirty-year career of coming down hard on bad guys by booting two thousand convicted criminals out of the county jail and into army tents behind razor wire, has just been startled by eight ounces of caramel-colored kitten.

"It won't bite, will it?" says Sheriff Joe Arpaio, flinching from the handful of cat thrust at him by a Maricopa County Sheriff's Office Animal Safe Hospice (MASH) unit officer. "I'm a dog man, you know," he says, regaining some of his composure but still warily holding the kitten away from his chest, where a gold tie tack in the shape of an automatic pistol gleams. "I hate cats," he grumbles.

The kitten looks up at him and squeaks. He looks down at her, then accusingly at the MASH officer. "Hey, whaddya feed her? She's thin!" he bellows.

Joe Arpaio, sheriff of Maricopa County, Arizona, with one of the rescued kittens housed in the jail he devotes to unwanted animals.

In 2001, a gang in Ahwatukee, a Phoenix suburb, killed and mutilated a dozen cats as part of an initiation ritual. That did it for Sheriff Joe, who may not like cats but is a hard-shelled guy with a gooey center when it comes to creatures.

"We didn't pull any punches," he says. "We blitzed the area. I formed an animal protection crew, six investigators. I go after animal abuse because it leads to murder. That executive at Del Monte who was killed by three teens? The guy who did the shooting had just burned three cats to death." Now a fleet of police vans bears the message: Help Sheriff Joe Stop Animal Abuse—Call (602) 876-1681. "And everybody arrested for animal abuse, we put them on the Web," he says.

Sheriff Joe is one of those men whose contents exceed his packaging. He is intense and compact, a large presence in a smallish frame, with dark eyes behind large glasses and a manner that is a mix of menace and charm. He is the son of Italian immigrants, and his mother died when he was born. He grew up in Springfield, Massachusetts, and his speech retains the East Coast wise-guy cadence; he speeds on, almost never pausing to inhale.

"We kicked out three hundred inmates and use this cell block for dogs and cats," he says. "The inmates eat at 3:00 a.m. and 5:00 p.m., the cheapest meals in history, twenty-five thousand meals a day. We spend a dollar a day on a dog and thirty cents a day to feed *her*," he says, gesturing at a young woman in the gray-striped jail uniform of the Maricopa County Jail trusty. How does he do that, we ask?

"We got ways," says Sheriff Joe in a tone that precludes further questions. "The food is disgusting; it's awful," says the woman, a MASH unit shift worker. "Yeah? Well don't come back here then!" Sheriff Joe retorts.

Not long ago, Maricopa County Jail reached a record population of ninety-five hundred inmates. Faced with severe overcrowding in the main jail, Sheriff Joe raised a city of tents (with heaters, fan, cement floors, and unlimited blankets—he points out) on the outskirts of downtown, masked by twelve-foot razor wire and trees.

"Our troops in Iraq aren't living in air conditioning; I don't see why the convicted felons should have better conditions than our troops," says Sheriff Joe. We don't argue.

"And they were watching cable TV and porn movies in the jail," he says. "We went to the Disney channel, the Weather Channel, the ten-part series on government, and three G-rated movies: *Old Yeller, Donald Duck,* and *Lassie Come Home.* That's it."

If Sheriff Joe has been harsh with the guilty, he has been no less gentle with the innocent—the animals that end up in the MASH unit. Inside the four-storey fortress that is the old First Avenue Maricopa County Jail, the harsh clang of heavy, blue metal doors is now softened with the whistles of cockatiels. Stark corridors, where a guard used to patrol every twenty-five minutes, have been painted with flowers, each inscribed with the names of animals rescued and passed to new owners: Sammy, Brittney, Jen, Cappy, Misty, Tom, Bud, Paws, Blaze, Sissy.

The halls are Purr Lane, Trustee Crossing, Bow Wow Way, and Second Chance Circle. For now, the MASH unit is home to twelve dogs, forty-six cats, two ferrets, and one exuberant cockatiel, a population that shifts constantly as new animals arrive and existing ones are placed with families. They have the run of cells that once held eight men each but were meant for half that number, furnished only with metal racks for bunks and a combination toilet and sink.

Bags, cans, and boxes of donated pet food cram the former visiting room. When an animal is adopted, it departs spayed or neutered, vaccinated, and with forty pounds of food and a leash and collar in hot pink—the color favored by Sheriff Joe, who found that dyeing things electric pink deterred inmates from walking away with county-issued underwear, towels, blankets, socks, and sweatshirts.

Here in cell no. 7, four kittens nurse at the side of their contented, sleepy, gray tabby mother. "This is the lockdown [isolation] cell. We'd never go in there unless we had three or four officers, because if you opened the door,

Tom Gilmore supervises the prison's ranch animal facility; inmates prize the opportunity to care for animals such as this Arabian stallion seized by police in a raid on a meth lab at a ranch.

you knew the fight was on," says Lieutenant Dave Williams, who started the MASH unit with Sheriff Joe in 2000.

"The animals are victims of abuse, neglect, and failure to have medical care," Dave explains. "Some are left behind in apartments to die. We've gone into houses and found dead puppies."

"We teach female inmates how to deal with pitchfork wounds, gunshots, burns, and ticks in the ear canals," Dave explains. "They clean cages, brush and exercise the animals, and give them a proper diet. They learn to get a dog to take a pill; they clean around chest tubes and treat skin rashes. When they leave here, they can go to PetSmart, feed stores, and area vet clinics, and when they show a training certificate from us, they get hired. The animals win; the inmates win."

"We screen them and see that they have a plan for life after jail. This program teaches girls to care for something instead of selling drugs."

"A lot of the girls get done with their court case the same time as the animals, and they sometimes adopt them," says Dave. "One girl adopted a Dalmatian named Pungo, and he goes to work with her at a vet clinic every day."

Dave expects that MASH units will match or exceed the improvements shown by the jail's Alpha Program (chemical addiction treatment), which reduced recidivism from 64 percent to 17 percent.

Law enforcement has good reason to take animal abuse seriously, he points out. "David Berkowitz's first victim was his neighbor's Labrador, and Jeffrey Dahmer and others hurt animals before they went on to hurt humans," he says. "Where animal abuse takes place, chances are domestic violence and child abuse are going on in the home too."

Many of the cats, dogs, birds, and ferrets in the MASH unit are on "courtesy holds"—kept safe for women fleeing domestic violence who have sought sanctuary in shelters. The women may retrieve their pets when they find a safe, stable home. To turn pets over to the pound or shelters exposes the animals to angry partners or husbands who have been known to go to the pound or humane society, get the animals out, and torture or kill them. And the threat to their pets is one lever that propels women to finally leave dangerous home situations.

"With many women, it's 'You can hurt me, but don't mess with my kids or animals,'" says Thelda Williams, the division commander of inmate programs. "It's a very powerful tool."

What happens to a pet when its owners are arrested? "Some animals hide under the bed and starve to death if no one else knows they are there, and some are removed to shelters or pounds," she says. "And if they are not claimed in three days, they may be put to sleep—that's horrendous."

"Sheriff Joe wanted this service, because he's aware that a lot of women know if they leave the pets behind, the pets will become victims," she says. "We keep them sixty days free of charge in the jail, and longer if the woman stays in touch with us."

Animals may also provide living evidence of crime. Last week, Dave tells us, a woman brought her bulldog to MASH because she was entering a shelter. The vet tech noticed the dog's mouth had what looked like cigarette burns, and the woman displayed the same signs. "So she questioned the woman," says Thelda. "She admitted her husband had put cigarettes to both of them and tried to poison both of them, but the woman wasn't willing to press charges against the husband. So we may not get him for domestic violence, but we may get him for animal abuse, and in Arizona, that's a felony. To think she had stayed that long, it crushes your heart to hear things like that. At least we could help her and the dog."

However the jail has been transformed, it's still a jail. And it feels wonderful to step out of the close and echoing building. We drive out of downtown Phoenix with Dave Williams. Ten minutes into the desert to the west of the jail, the MASH II outdoor unit houses rescued large animals, including hogs, roosters, sheep, pigs, and goats. They come from ranches where they were starved, beaten, or neglected, or where their owners were arrested for running methamphetamine labs and there was no one left on the property to care for them.

For now, as they await their owners' court cases, there are twenty-six horses in the shady pipe stalls, including six stallions and one miniature mule named Jack. They are bay, paint, and roan, gleaming, and on the chubby side thanks to excellent hay and brushing lavished on them by male inmates.

Tom Gilmore, a lean, middle-aged cowboy with an outsized roping-champ buckle on his belt, directs MASH II. Caring for rescued horses and other animals is a plum job for inmates, says Tom. "They turn in a tank order—a jail request form—then I go and interview them," he explains. "I ask 'em if they've been around horses or livestock, if they are afraid of it. If they want to and are willing to work, they can learn something. Out here there are a lotta horse outfits, and after release, they can apply to help maintain the horses, do feedin' and cleanin' and general maintenance. One former inmate works in a feed store."

"The sheriff tries to tell everybody he doesn't have a soft spot, but he does," says Tom, who once persuaded Sheriff Joe to kiss Jack the mule on the nose for a photo. "He's not a horse person and is kind of afraid of them, but he has a soft spot for animals."

The horse pens are just across the road from the tent city. That's where Tina McFalls lives when she is not working in the MASH unit. Tina is coming to the end of a six-month sentence for selling crystal methamphetamine and for criminal impersonation.

"I'm a drug addict. I'll fight with that the rest of my life," she admits. "On the drugs you are a different person; you don't have responsibility."

Although she is looking forward to air conditioning and a soft bed, she doesn't want to leave the dogs and cats. "I love them all; they all have big hearts; I want to take them all home," she says. "No matter what you say or wear or look like, they love you automatically. It's wonderful to get to come to work and give your love to them and they give it back to you—it's excellent."

"We have animals that been locked in the yard without food, some are full of ticks, some are burned, some dogs were sexually abused," she says. "One pit bull mix, you couldn't go into the room without her tearing you apart if she got the chance. Now she's a big ol' love bug. It took her a little while. I get down on the floor with them all and let them lick and jump all over me, and none of them hurt me even though they have been hurt and abused."

When she graduated from high school in a suburb of Detroit, Tina wanted to be a mom. She married but never had children. Now at age thirty-five, she is on the floor playing with MASH kittens named Cuddles, Cindy, Olivia, Johnny, and Brandon. And she has responsibility for Labradors, mutts, pit bulls, pit bull mixes, and the MASH unit's latest addition, a Jack Russell terrier named Clarissa.

"Me and children get along perfect. Me and animals get along good; the reaction you get from them is just like a child," she says. "Some of the animals are scared at first; they have been beaten and they're skittish. When they see, hey, this person's not gonna harm me, they play and give me love back. All animals here are great. If you take the time with them and show them love, they give it right back to you."

When she is released, Tina hopes to find a job as a veterinary assistant. "I got tools now and can do what I need to do and be a better person than what I was," she says confidently. "They got great officers here. They deal with you as person instead of a criminal. They don't treat you like garbage. They give you an opportunity to prove who you are." Tina liked the work at MASH so well she has requested to do the remainder of her sentence— seventy-five hours of community service—in the unit.

"I'm learning a lot, and they are willing to teach me. If you do something you love, you give 110 percent," she says. "This is an excellent program. Here I've learned unconditional love without having to be high."

7

ENOUGH IS ENOUGH

DON MARRO AND LILLIAN CLANCY AND THEIR DOGS

FOUR ARKS HAVE come to rest in the front parlor of the 1919 red brick mansion on a rise in the Virginia hills. Set against cyclamen-pink walls and pistachio-green woodwork, the front room teems with model pandas, whales, moose, caribou, toucans, and horses silently marching to safety up the ramps of the wooden ships.

In the hallways, a motley pack of dogs—big dogs, enthusiastic dogs, barking, growling dogs—swirl and skitter around Don Marro, who appears kind of tall and growly himself. "We have more dogs than sense," says Lillian Clancy, his wife, who is slight, with gray, bobbed hair and a pink outdoorswoman's face. "There are sixteen dogs here, ten indoors and six outdoors. Two outdoor dogs are blind, as are two of the indoor dogs. Our friend John says that driving by here with all the dogs outside reposing on the front lawn is like watching the lions on the Serengeti."

Fortunately, we have arrived at mealtime: in the sunlit kitchen off the parlor, twelve-foot walls are festooned with framed paintings of cows, tapirs, pigs, sheep, and chickens, and sixteen large pastel bowls are laid out

Don Marro and Lillian Clancy of Virginia take in abandoned dogs and lobby for legislative change to stop overbreeding and to make affordable spay and neuter services available. "Dogs give us an opportunity to improve humanity," says Don.

on a butcher block. A white cat sleeps in the sunbeam, and a commercial-size soup pot simmers on the stove.

"Bones for the outdoor dogs—to keep them busy, they get one every day," explains Lillian, ladling bones and broth onto the vitamins and medication in the rainbow of bowls. There is the scrape of claws on the back stairs, and a large black dog growls on the landing above the kitchen. "Come on, honey, sweetie, no one is going to take your food," Lillian calls to a skeptical Labrador mix named Lacey.

As the pack romps and roves the rooms, Don recounts their histories: Howard, a Doberman mix, was hit by a car and his owners left him to die. George, a basset hound, came wandering to their house, unkempt and going blind. Lobo was saved from a shelter. Eddie was found wandering the freeway median.

"And that painting is Angel Annie," says Don, indicating a dog portrait near the stove. "She was dumped by somebody who was angry that she was older at the end of her life than at the beginning."

Don is a doer. He got tractor trailers banned from the stretch of Highway 17 that runs between Route 66 and Route 50 at the Ashby Gap, not only reducing noise and pollution in the historic valley of Virginia's Blue Ridge Mountains but also stopping almost all of the loss of life—human and animal—from speeding tractor-trailer trucks.

He and Lillian are now tackling a tragedy on an even larger scale. "Animal shelters in the commonwealth of Virginia kill 135,000 dogs and cats a year," says Don. "The reason is the disposability mindset, no population control, no other cultural tradition. And it's killing, not euthanasia. A state that can't feed its children properly, educate them effectively, or balance a budget consistently nevertheless is content to spend $62 million on handling and killing pets," he says.

"Most animal welfare groups focus on ways to devote enough money and time to rescue dogs, but no state official funds the effort to correct overpopulation."

Don starts at intense and gets more so as he speaks. His gray beard and hair, high arched brows, New York accent, and sure speech coalesce in a picture of tough, smart fury. "And there are a number of people who breed dogs for evil purposes, or just extra money. They sell puppies at Christmas, breed them to fight, breed them then kill the excess inventory or used up breeding stock. This is incredible. If we don't license, regulate and tax breeders there is no accountability, no consequences."

"It's part of farm culture that reacts to pet breeding regulation as stifling, a slippery slope," says Don.

Don and Lillian began helping animals in need when they lived in San Francisco, where he worked in computer software, and she ran an executive search firm specializing in biotechnology companies. Their first rescue was Bruno, a Doberman with a broken leg. It's a family calling: their daughter Elizabeth Ross took part in preventing the U.S. Air Force from sending its space exploration chimpanzees to testing laboratories. "It's her life's work to make change too," says Lillian.

Don and Lillian believe "you need to be responsible for every animal you give life to." Their attempt to introduce legislation to raise license fees and tax breeders to fund wide-scale spay and neuter services failed, but they plan to reintroduce it next session. "Inertia defeats it," says Don, "the same lazy and defective logic that excluded women from the right to vote and kept people in bondage. Today those things are regarded as unconscionable, but there are other dark chapters still, the Holocaust or 'ethnic cleansing,' for example. There has to be some catalyst that triggers outrage, some threshold event, to say enough is enough."

Don has long since had enough. He is big, smart, fearless, and furious. And he and Lillian are ferociously organized. Through their group, Virginia Voters for Animal Welfare, they craft, introduce, and track legislation on pet breeding, owner education, pet and breeder licensing, and pet euthanasia methods. There are times when Don would like to act more directly. "I know of a dog that survived a lethal injection at the pound, and the guy stuffed a hose down its throat and drowned it," he says, his eyes darkening. "That creep should get hosed himself."

We pile into his van to tour their land, to give Don a chance to decompress while freeing Lillian to feed the pack. To the north of the antebellum-style house are a fenced orchard of fruit trees and raised beds of a large garden. To the west, on the gentle slope of the Blue Ridge Mountains, the stable and adjoining paddocks have been converted to kennels. Brenda and Alice, mixed-breed brindle puppies, dash around the paddock to greet us. And Rosemary, a blind golden retriever mix, barks as we drive by. We round a curve and a small rise, and Don recounts another rescue.

"Gordon was a bluetick hound mix who was kept in a cage so small he couldn't stand up, and when he was rescued, he had to learn to walk, to run, to bark. He had spinal problems and trouble in his back legs, and he did not have much time. It was the greatest joy to me and to him when he learned he could roll on his back in the grass. Finally, he couldn't climb stairs anymore. And there are a lot of stairs in our house. My bedroom is on the second floor. On the day before he died, I found him up there; he had made it all the way up those stairs to see me."

"This is Gordon's place," and he points to crocuses and forsythia blooming among rocks. "It motivates you; it makes you sad," he says. "You gotta take care of those who depend on us, who don't know better. What kind of morality would willingly allow this killing and cruelty to continue?"

Don and Lillian already stopped death on this road in the historic valley beyond their gates. If they succeed with their new legislation, they may forever improve Virginia state law for animals, setting a national precedent.

There are things, however, they can't control. When we are out of Don's earshot, Lillian lowers her voice and tells us, "Don has spinal stenosis and neuropathy; he can't feel his feet. We are moving to a different house because he can't climb stairs easily anymore."

For Don and Lillian, time is crucial now, and time is even more precious with their animals. "Dogs give us an opportunity to improve humanity," says Don. "Animals are happy. Emotionally, it's like a runner's endorphin rush to be with them. On a metaphysical level, they add a meaning in life."

This is where Don and Lillian have chosen to make a difference, for the good of animals on a large and small scale. "This is how society improves, when people care: about freeing slaves, about giving women the vote, about ethical standards," says Don. "This is people who make changes. This is social evolution."

Epilogue

In 2008, the Virginia General Assembly banned gas chambers for pet euthanasia, curtailed puppy-mill operations and placed them under scrutiny and state regulation, and increased penalties for dogfighting, including making it a RICO offense punishable by at least five years incarceration and a million dollar fine.

Faerie Fleur simply showed up in their house on the sofa one morning, joining Don and Lillian's pack of formerly homeless dogs.

Chuck and Sue Thoreson have structured their lives to care for unwanted, crippled horses, dogs dumped in the country, and castaway cats. One cat—a formerly feral barn kitten named Emma—repaid their love by doting on Sue's mother throughout her life and keeping vigil through her last illness.

8

SUCH DEAR FRIENDS

CHUCK AND SUE THORESON AND THEIR ANIMAL FAMILY

"COME ON, KIDS!" Chuck and Sue Thoreson call, heading down the driveway with the family for a walk. Behind them runs little bowlegged Gauss, a tricolored Shih Tzu named for an eighteenth-century mathematician. He is followed by roly-poly Sophie, a speckled Labrador cross; Chum, a café-au-lait-colored poodle-terrier cross; Chelsea, a pale cocoa standard poodle; and Babington, a plump white cat. They swerve and dart off the trail, hop, skitter, and pant, and look adoringly at Mom and Dad. Chuck carries a small brass hunting horn and blows random toots to encourage the distracted among the group to keep up.

Back on the Thoresons' farmhouse porch, the shrewd Emma, a calico cat with a limp, and a small, gray tiger-striped cat, Portia, still sleek and shiny at seventeen, watch from a sunny step.

"Dumped in the country" is the refrain when the Thoresons explain how they built their animal family. Fortunately the country was near Rise Over Run Farm, their farm in western Minnesota. "Chelsea is the only dog we purchased since we were married thirty-two years ago; the rest were found," says Sue.

Sophie was a six-month-old pup. Chuck and Sue suspect somebody took her out hunting, didn't like her performance, and abandoned her in the woods. Sue found Gauss, muddy and matted with burrs, crouched under a mailbox on a hot July day. And Portia arrived in a load of hay.

There are also nineteen horses on the farm, mostly Thoroughbreds no longer able to race, breed, or be ridden. Bay and black, gray and roan, they stroll the paddocks and sun themselves in loafing sheds. It takes Sue or Chuck more than an hour to concoct and serve the special diets for their elderly horses, and still more time to administer medications. Sue's beloved first horse, Whiff, died recently at thirty-two, his life and comfort prolonged by daily nutritional cocktails of glucosamine, chondroitin, and hyaluronic acid. "I don't begrudge them a moment," says Sue, who has nursed as many as thirty horses at one time.

Chuck is a retired math teacher in the grip of a golf mania—he plays daily in good weather. Sue still commutes to the Twin Cities, where she runs the 401(k) plan for a large health-care organization.

"We can't travel because of all the animals," Sue says, looking a little wistful. "Aging horses, dogs, and cats need meds. And we ended up working more years, because we spend a lot of money on them. But we wouldn't do this unless there was a lot of enjoyment. So the house gets dirty—they're still a joy."

Fortunately, Chuck and Sue have created a welcoming place to stay home with their big family. They remodeled their late-nineteenth-century clapboard house, adding a white kitchen with granite countertops, a dining room with French doors leading to a deck, and a woodstove in the front parlor. Photos of their racing Thoroughbreds decorate the back hall, and the living-room walls are lined with bookshelves stacked with equestrian art and books by Walter Farley, Marguerite Henry, Will James, Rudyard Kipling, and A. A. Milne.

When they first married, Sue explains, they were living in a townhouse with four stray cats, which gave Chuck a horrible time with his asthma and allergies. They chose to keep the cats, defy the allergies, and bought ten acres in the country. Between the barns and the house, they now have six cats. "We would have more, but the resident cats won't let them integrate," Sue explains.

And then they added Emma. Her mother was a feral cat that gave birth in a hay shed, but when Sue noticed her kittens were disappearing one by one (meals for tomcats or skunks, she guesses), she brought her into the house and nursed her with feline formula. Young kittens not only need to be fed but also stroked every three hours in order to urinate, so Sue parked Emma with her mother, Lois, for kitty day care.

"One day I put her in a kennel to protect her from our poodles, and when I came home, the dogs had gone at the kennel and dragged it by the heating pad cord, and Emma was missing part of her paw," Sue says. "She was so traumatized, and now she couldn't function as a farm cat."

Emma the farm cat became Lois's cat. Lois had suffered from severe bipolar depression all her life, and Sue (an only child) recalls her mother spending hours in a darkened room. "When I was a kid, Mom didn't know what she had, and neither did her doctors," says Sue. "It showed up as migraines, stomachaches, and back problems. When she got older, what it actually was became more apparent. Mom's depression was so bad, she became immobilized, and Emma and Fritz, her schnauzer, were her constant companions."

Years later, when Lois decided to forgo treatment for kidney failure, she moved into Rise Over Run Farm, bringing Emma with her. Emma never left her bedside for the week that Lois slept, slipped into a coma, and died. Emma the cat had made a commitment to Lois, and she kept it.

People need to be that reciprocal, too, the Thoresons believe. "We need to educate that a pet is a lifelong commitment similar to a child, because you are responsible for their well-being," says Sue. "People as a species are not the greatest. Their treatment of animals is better than it was, but it is slow to improve."

"People are more delicate and difficult, and our relationships are more tenuous," Sue muses. "With people you have to be so careful. Animals take you as you are. They are nonjudgmental, just happy you are there, good company. They're such dear friends."

"And animals are very tactile," she adds, as Gauss wiggles up against her on the sofa and gives a crackly growl that Sue assures us is a dog version of a purr. That blissful mutual touch extends to bedtime too. With part of their pack sharing their bed every night, sometimes the Thoresons get displaced. "I slept on the floor once; it was so crowded and one dog was not well," Sue says with a laugh. It's the sort of thing any mom would do. "If I'd had a child, I'd feel not one iota different about animals. Maybe I'd have less time, but I'd feel no different about them."

9

FEARSOMELY ATTUNED

BJ ANDERSEN, TERESA MCKENZIE, AND THEIR DOG, LIBBY

WE ARE HEADED up into the villages of Sublimity, Stayton, and Scio in the foothills of the Oregon Cascades, which boast a climate so moist that moss sprouts even on concrete curbs and lichen seems to inexorably consume everything that doesn't move. This is small-farm, medium-ranch, and big trail-riding country. Horses, llamas, and alpacas graze in small, lush pastures bordered by druidic-looking cedars, ditches thick with dormant sword ferns, and fields of neatly sheared rows of future Christmas trees. At a local tack shop and feed mill, pale pink, green, and blue lariats are coiled on the walls, and snap-button western shirts are for sale along with rifle scabbards, rain ponchos, and waterproof saddlebags.

Chalky plum-colored brambles form arches along the road, which winds upward past vineyards and pollarded fruit trees and nut trees, their trunks grizzled with lichens.

It's February, and snow gleams on the clear-cut meadows at higher altitudes, while in the valley below us, golfers are moving across squelchy greens.

BJ Andersen and her partner, Teresa McKenzie, moved to one of these farms because of their love for animals and their compulsion to help those in harm's way.

Teresa is running the tractor, grading a load of gravel on their new driveway when I cross the mud on boards that span their unfinished front yard to meet them. First I have to maneuver past a Jetta with a "My Dog is Smarter than Your Honor Student" bumper sticker and a second one proclaiming "My SUV Has Four Legs, a Mane, a Tail and It Doesn't Guzzle Gas."

BJ, attended by three dogs, crosses the vast deck that wraps their cheerful, sage-green home "designed for people with seasonal affective disorder, that's why all the windows," she quips.

Libby is glossy black, more border collie than Labrador in size, with a graying muzzle and distinctive cowlicks running the length of her spine. She greets me with a plush hippo toy, her amber eyes alight with an intelligence as profound as that of a chimpanzee. "Where's your duck?" BJ asks, as we settle in armchairs in the generous, sunlit living room. Libby drops the hippo, trots to a basket of dog toys, and retrieves a plush grouse. "Oh, alright, it's got wings. I suppose that's close enough."

"She is so stinkin' smart," laughs BJ, "she watches what I do and figures ways to help." Figuring out how to help seems to be Libby's calling. Not long ago, BJ was taking care of an elkhound-husky mix, and visiting a lakeside central Oregon lodge. It was midwinter after sunset, and BJ was in a bunkhouse behind the lodge and away from the lake. Libby ran barking to the lodge where some men were barbecuing dinner, then began running to the edge of the small frozen lake.

"They had watched *Lassie* often enough to know they should follow her," she says. "When they got to the lake, they found the husky had fallen through the ice. She had tried to climb out, but her wet forelegs froze to the surface, and she hung there in the icy lake. Libby got the two men to come see the problem, and they maneuvered until they could hang off the end of the dock and grab her collar. Much longer and that dog would have died

BJ Andersen and her perfect animal partner, Libby, live on a farm in the foothills of Oregon's Cascade range. Libby saved one dog from freezing in a lake and another from dying in the wilderness.

of hypothermia. She wasn't barking, and no one would have known until it was too late." That rescue earned Libby the Diamond Collar Award in the category of "animal rescuing animal" from the Portland Humane Society at a gala pets and people party.

Helping BJ is Libby's primary mission, which BJ intimates is not a coincidence. From Libby's records, she was born the day BJ's older brother died of AIDS. "After he passed, I decided I was ready to have a dog," she explains. "I was thirty-five and never had one as an adult. When my brother died, that meant bedrock change. My sense of identity was I have *this* number of siblings and *this* number of parents. I lost who I was."

BJ selected Libby at the Oregon Humane Society in Portland, where the nine-week-old puppy had been surrendered as part of an unwanted litter. Perhaps her shy temperament had worked against her—she was the last one left. The puppy's initial reserve, however, attracted BJ.

"She was not particularly outgoing; she hung out at the back of the kennel," she recalls. "I was planning on adopting an adult dog so I wouldn't have to deal with puppy issues, but I took her into a meet-and-greet room, and there was a loud noise somewhere, and she dove into my lap. I thought, okay, this is a being that thinks of me as a safe place."

Libby was a huge step for BJ, much bigger than getting a dog. She was finally ready to commit to something for the rest of her life. "She's amazingly the right puppy for me," she says. "If she were a needy, high-maintenance dog, I wouldn't have survived. From her I got a level of commitment I was also finally ready to make."

Putting down roots on this ridge top with the view of Richardson Gap is part of a commitment she had never made before either. Photos of the Andersen family's five previous homes—beginning with a rented cottage—decorate the dining-room wall of this latest house, which BJ and Theresa share with BJ's mother, Nancy, and father, Arland, who is retired from the family-owned construction business.

The family also includes Legend, a young black-and-white border-collie and rottweiler mix, who capers up, snapping his jaws in a playful, conversational way, and an elderly bobtailed Australian shepherd named Dee O Gee, who bumps against my knees and gives me a soulful look.

Libby and Legend escort us around the property, which was head-high in poison oak and blackberries until the women took a bulldozer to it, clearing the choked land back to its natural balance of oak and fir. BJ points out checker mallow, buttercup, columbine, and Douglas fir bearded with lichen, while Libby scouts earnestly for mice and rabbits.

Their horses are mostly rescues: Sky and Ed are foals from a PMU ranch (PMU, or pregnant mare urine, is the chief component of hormone replacement therapy for women. Large herds of mares are kept pregnant and stand in collection barns, where tubing funnels their urine to a tank. Foals are sold off at three months and the mares rebred); Blackberry and Juniper are mustang rescues; and Ochoco, another rescued golden mustang with a dreadlock mane and ground-sweeping tail, is being bullied gently around the pasture by Zephyr, BJ's curvaceous bay Lipizzan-Clydesdale cross. A miniature stallion, seventeen-year-old Jupiter, looking like a bay burr in his winter coat, nickers to us in the hopes of getting hay. The horses are part of BJ's long-term plan to partly subsidize her rescued menagerie through training horses and riders in natural horsemanship (a philosophy of working with horses through communication techniques that build a partnership with the animal rather than dominating it) and by selling the modestly priced horses to good new homes.

For a few minutes, we watch Teresa running the tractor—like BJ, she is middle-aged, trim, and silver-haired. Under her baseball cap, Teresa's face has a striking, androgynous beauty. "I thought Richard Gere was handsome until I saw her," says BJ.

"What does Libby give BJ?" I ask Teresa.

"Everything," says Teresa.

Libby is BJ's first dog, and Teresa is the first person she's ever settled down with. "Before her, I'd never had a relationship more permanent than with a cat," says BJ. "I bond wherever I go, but ask me to commit for the rest of my life, and I wouldn't make it. I was always reinventing myself, and I never expected a person to keep up with me, let alone an animal."

The reinvention included two stints as a college student (a self-described compulsive learner, BJ has a degree in equestrian studies, with later schooling in religious philosophy, environmental studies, and art), two years in AmeriCorps, several years caretaking a YWCA camp, and somewhere along the way, a couple of years as a Buddhist nun.

"The hardest thing about being a Buddhist nun was giving up my two cats," she admits. "I had to give up everything in my life to devote to a life of service to others. People you can break up with and they understand, but you can't break up with animals."

Currently, she works in another dimension of service to others as kennel manager at the Willamette Humane Society in Salem, Oregon. Some twelve thousand unwanted animals pour through the shelter each year, and BJ credits Libby for giving her the confidence she needs to handle the job. The dog is a partner when it comes to the part of BJ's work that involves temperament testing, and BJ's belief in the fantastic qualities of shelter dogs came from Libby.

Libby's opinion can mean life or death for some of those unwanted dogs. "We do temperament testing on dogs that come in," BJ explains. "We test them around food, other dogs, and in situations with people to see how they react, how adoptable they might be. Libby sends calming signals to the dogs; she de-escalates their anxiety and stress."

"She's so appropriate and so accurate that if a dog will respond to her, then we know that's a dog we can work with; it just needs to be taught some ways and boundaries. When we have a difficult or borderline dog, she is our expert."

Libby's sense of responsibility came in handy not long ago when BJ was caring for a friend's newly-adopted Doberman-rottweiler mix. "We were out felling trees for firewood, which scared the dog and she went piling out of the truck," says BJ. "Libby saw I was wound up, figured out I was trying to find the dog and started down the dirt road, sweeping like a scent-tracking dog. The friend and I followed her."

The road became a trail, the trail vanished, and the panic-stricken city dog disappeared in the jungle-like Oregon Coast Range. The women, following Libby, tracked the runaway dog for a mile and a half before they could catch her. "That dog would have died in the wilderness, but Libby figured out she could help," says BJ.

Living and working in the Oregon woods, BJ stays in the moment with her dog. "With people, I can get all conceptual and not really there. With Libby, I stay present, very grounded in a companionable silence of sharing the greater-than-human world."

"Some beings are more sentient than others, and she's so stinkin' sentient," says BJ fondly. "There was a hole in my family, and I was okay with the psychological replacement. We are fearsomely attuned."

Libby is "border-collie smart with a pause button" says BJ. She has given BJ the confidence and skills to perform the job of kennel manager at a humane society.

As a child, Drew Fitzpatrick ran away from home to escape abuse. She now shelters rescued horses, goats, and sheep at a small farm through her Minnesota Hooved Animal Rescue Foundation.

10

DREW'S EDEN

DREW FITZPATRICK AND HER MINNESOTA HOOVED ANIMAL
RESCUE FOUNDATION

WHEN DREW FITZPATRICK'S daughter was eighteen months old, her husband issued an ultimatum. "He told me I had an unnatural fixation with horses and that I had to make a decision: them or him," she says. "I had known my mare for way longer than him, so it wasn't hard. 'Don't let the door hit you in the ass,' I said."

Horses have captivated Drew ever since she can remember. She was still sucking her thumb when she kicked her pony-ring mount into a trot at a local grocery store opening. Her parents divorced when she was five, and her mother remarried, but Drew hung on to her love of horses.

At ten, she watched as her pony, Major Dundee, was sold to neighbors down the road. Not long after that, Major Dundee accidentally escaped from his pasture. "And he was hit by the school bus," says Drew, blowing a tight stream of cigarette smoke. "It broke his neck and legs, but he was still alive, and I was helpless. The people who had bought him were right there, and they said it was our pony; they didn't want to take responsibility for what had happened. They didn't care about the suffering of the animal. I had to go to school, and he was screaming and thrashing, and nobody would claim ownership, and the other kids were teasing me because I had to go to school and my pony was screaming. The cops had to shoot him."

Life did not improve for Drew after that. At fourteen, she encountered the naked, decapitated, and decomposed body of a girlfriend in a cornfield. Her stepfather told her it should have been Drew and continued to beat her. She went to school with black eyes and concussions. Teachers noticed, but the one who spoke up was threatened with the loss of her job by Drew's stepfather. There was no help, no social worker, in her small Minnesota town.

At fifteen, Drew knew that to save her life she had to leave home, even if it meant abandoning her horses. She hitchhiked east and south, living on the beach of Padre Island, Texas, and the streets of various big cities. "I didn't seek aid from anyone; I just kept movin'," she says. "I found different ways of surviving on the road, sometimes by begging, and sometimes I went hungry 'cause I didn't like that. I didn't resort to anything unsavory like prostitution. One time I strung beads with a whole bunch of street kids in a little basement room, and I remember being really friggin' hungry. I hated it and made enough money to get out of there."

Things got worse. She ate road kill. "I cooked it as best I could, but it was eat a fox or forget it, so I ate a gray fox. It was nasty; they taste terrible. You can always find ketchup packets, but it makes the worst soup; it makes you throw up. I could've gone home, but I wasn't gonna; I would have got the hell beat out of me. I was just too stubborn."

In New York, she managed the mailroom for a sixties radical underground newspaper, the *Yipster Times,* and occasionally went riding on livery horses in Central Park. Tom, the founder of the newspaper and of *High Times,* an alternative magazine, staked her to five Arabian horses that they planned to train and sell. But when Tom committed suicide, Drew fled with her horses from New York to central Florida and got a job on a horse farm. At one point she rented a stable, training horses and living in the hayloft where the only plumbing was a garden hose.

She returned to Minnesota and was married briefly, but mostly she and her daughter survived on Drew's horse-training jobs and other work: waitressing, dog grooming, driving a delivery truck, selling plants. For five years, she fitted shoes and appliances to diabetics and made braces for injured horses on the side.

Today she has a small Eden of her own making, the Minnesota Hooved Animal Rescue Foundation, a ten-acre farm in Zimmerman, Minnesota. Fantail pigeons dance in the sunbeams where a black frizzle rooster holds court in the open barn door of the farm. In the hayloft above them, Drew's friend Randy, who sports a long gray beard and a tattoo of a wizard on his bicep, tosses fragrant hay bales down into the yard. Arabians, quarter horses, mixed-breed horses, and a Percheron colt mill and snooze in pastures and pens. Two donkeys—stubby, gray Joseph and tall, creamy Beatrice—demand dinner, shrieking like dissonant clarinets.

A pair of sheep named Sven and Baabette, a Jersey cow named Jessifer and her Guernsey cow friend Clover, and a peacock and his ivory pea hen eat, drift around, or doze in the sun. "Baabette fell off or escaped a slaughter truck, we think, and appeared in a neighborhood where dogs chased her, so I took her," says Drew, introducing us to her flock. "And Sven I bought at an auction for two dollars when he was a couple days' old and nobody wanted a bottle lamb," she continues, rubbing the wooly lamb's ear. "I raised him in the house with my dogs. Talk about 'Mary Had a Little Lamb.' This one would curl up on the pickup seat with me, and we'd go to the bank and the store."

We follow Drew into the barn, where she clips an X-ray of one of Beatrice's hooves to a screen. The hoof curves upward and curls back like a ram's horn. "Beatrice was lying down most of the time, because she couldn't walk on her neglected hooves, so we took a Sawz-All and whacked the foot like this first," Drew explains, drawing a diagonal line across the distorted hoof. Then the farrier reshaped the deformed hooves so that Beatrice could walk again. "In about forty-five minutes, they go from Turkish slippers to normal. They're sore because the tendons and muscles snap back into place, so we have to use all kinds of pain killers."

Drew is in her forties, with pale skin, hair, and eyes, and a limpid and remote stolidity that reminds me of Vermeer's *Girl with a Pearl Earring*. "I'm a real odd person, not touchy-huggy with people," she says, blowing a stream of cigarette smoke down the front of her flannel shirt. "I didn't fit in. We moved a lot; it was hard to make friends. Drew is an unusual name, and I got teased. Horses were a constant; they don't tease you or pick on you. If they don't like you, they just kick you. Horses are not as conniving and underhanded as people. People are too hard to figure out."

She went to a psychologist—once. "And in his waiting room was this painting, this egg all by itself on the rocks over here, and a coupla birds mating over here. It creeped me out. I went to him one time, said, 'See ya later,' and went and got a horse. I know what's good for me."

"Don't touch that fence; it's so hot you'll pee in your pants," she cautions, as I am venturing to scratch a mare through the electric wire corral fence in the center of the farmyard.

Drew has shaped her calling into a career of mopping up the wreckage from irresponsible, cruel, or damaged human beings, and soothing the hurt animals at their mercy. Her mission forces her into triage, into scenes where she has to be decisive, responsible, and merciful where others are not.

So Drew does the hard and the ugly rescues—going in with the sheriff to seize forty-five starving horses in Pine County (five more were already dead), and another sixteen starved horses in Todd County that were walking over the bodies of seven of the herd, including foals. She hauls horses to the university veterinary clinic for surgery and intensive care. She euthanizes horses that cannot be saved. And she carefully screens people who apply to adopt her recovered animals. "That means a lot of paperwork and people," she says. "I hate paperwork and people."

"Horses—I know what they are going to do, they do not try to kill themselves, they are predictable in their unpredictability. They are reasonable animals; people are not."

"I had to teach a cop how to shoot a horse the other night," she says, with little more visible emotion than she has shown when discussing anything else. "It had got onto the road and been hit by a car and had its leg torn off, and the owner was not there, and the vet wasn't getting there fast enough. The cop had never shot a horse before, and it was pretty emotional, but we were both bucking up 'cause that's what you do. Say 'Geez this sucks,' then deal with the body, deal with the traffic. It was horrible, but you know what? I'm glad I was able to be there to help. Who else would have gotten it euthanized that quickly? And it was good for me to get closure on the whole pony incident when I was a kid."

"That was how many years ago?" she wonders. "It's so frustrating and you feel so helpless when you are a child. I know what it's like to be not in control. I want to help these animals. They are total innocents; they are our dependents."

Drew loves all the animals that survive abuse and come to her farm, but she has, she admits, some favorites. "The animal that has been absolutely whupped down, thin, depressed, worried you are going to hit them, that's the animal I have the most affection for and spend the most time with until they come out of their shell," she says. "I can see their psyche uncurl. They make themselves a little vulnerable; they give you trust and trust you not to wreck it. It's most important they get someone who protects and nurtures that until they can really unfold and be normal and trust people."

She is rightfully fussy about who gets the animals she has repaired. "If a person doesn't understand that they have to take care of the psyche, they are not getting a horse from me," says Drew. "It's a hard, hard thing to adopt these animals out. If the people have barbed wire on their place, no adoption. It's my rules, my ball. All the horses are on my team. If you don't like it, go play somewhere else."

Not all the humans who hurt animals do so intentionally, she says. "People who are at the end of their ropes, like going through a divorce, if you talk some sense to them and be nice to them, if you say, 'I'm here to help you,' that's okay. They are fundamentally good anyway, just horribly stressed. They understand and say, 'Yes, please help my animals.' That's nice; I like doing that. But boy, the ones that are crazy are hard to deal with, and some need to have psych evaluations. We can order that as part of sentencing."

Drew was once called to a farm where a woman starved two horses—one to death. There were big ruts in the ground where the dying horse had continued to paddle and paddle, she says. Usually cool, Drew lost it this time. "And the other poor, skinny-ass horse with his head down was standing there lookin' at his friend's body . . . I just screamed, 'Your horse starved to death! Where's your goddamn hay?!' I ended up doing the schoolteacher thing with my finger: 'Shame on you!' I had her bawling. She signed a surrender form. And I put the horse in my trailer and drove away. The woman ended up in a mental care facility."

Drew sees humans relating to animals in roughly three ways: one is the old school, what she calls the animals-have-no-soul group, those who see animals as objects.

Others lavish attention and vet care on their creatures. "They are ethical and have enough money to take care of 'em, or if they don't, they at least don't have fifty bajillion animals," she says. "They see the world as a whole." In the middle are those whom Drew describes as "just attaining consciousness. They are getting into having animals and getting a puppy for their child, and the influences they bump into help to form their opinions about animals."

Some of the old school—those who regard animals as necessary and not much more—can change, says Drew. She's seen it happen. "I was telling my eighty-two-year-old grandmother what I see and do and why. And she said, 'All these years I've looked at animals the wrong way.' That was really cool. Dairy cows to her were just part of life, but when she was older and animals were a luxury, she slowed down and watched and enjoyed them. I don't know what makes people like that change, but you let them think it's their idea."

Her grandma's conversion notwithstanding, until every animal owner is kind, competent, and ethical, Drew's work will be needed. For now, she and the Rescue Foundation need much more help than she is able to afford on

"I know what it's like to be not in control," says Drew. "I want to help these animals. They are total innocents, they are our dependents."

her salary mending saddles and other tack at a local saddlery. Her fences break, her 1989 Ford truck is hemorrhaging oil, there are vet bills and feed bills. But just now, this morning, a rescued mare—one of five that survived in a starved herd of ten—has given birth.

"She dropped a gorgeous palomino filly foal," says Drew, squatting on the front steps of her white rambler home. Randy brings her a bouquet of dandelions. Drew chuckles. "I've mellowed; I'm not near so autistic," she says. "I've learned to relax, express myself. It hasn't been easy. Watching animals is what did it. How simply without guilt they express themselves, how forward they are, uncomplicated. They are happy within themselves. Horses don't brag; a horse that feels good can prance and everybody rejoices in that prancing horse. When they show you joy, you revel in it with them. I love these creatures—the pigeons, the cats, all of them."

11

CAN-DO CIMI

SMALL ROSETTES OF scar tissue—circles of pink, white, and bare black hide—still bloom on Cimmaron's hips and shoulders, the bedsore legacy of a trauma that few horses could survive and through which few owners would have stayed hopeful.

In 1986, Cimmaron, then a two-year-old colt, was en route to a Southern California training stable to begin his racing career. The young Thoroughbred had resisted getting into the trailer and was heavily tranquilized. As the truck raced down the highway, he fought the tie rope and flung himself upside down. His neck, still tied to the manger, was severely wrenched, and he sustained a concussion and a spinal cord injury. For a week he was half-conscious and rigid with pain while veterinarians tried anti-inflammatories, antibiotics, anything.

Unable to pay huge veterinary bills, and faced with a horse with limited prospects at best, his owner wanted him euthanized. Trainer Diana Thompson, who had done muscle massage and therapeutic touch on Cimmaron, persuaded him to relinquish the horse—and his bills—to her.

"Depression is a big part of disability, and riding lifts people's spirits," says Pegasus director Lori Sarner. "Here it's what they can do that counts."

She enlisted the help of vets for acupuncture and homeopathy, and twelve days after the accident, Cimmaron, with the help of a dozen people, rose to his feet and walked.

What he couldn't do was race again, although he could tolerate light riding. In 1992, Cimmaron was donated to the Pegasus Riding Academy for the Handicapped in Indio, California, and began giving mobility, hope, and fun to humans with injuries.

Pegasus is a little more than an acre of neatly raked and swept desert landscaped with petunias, rosemary, and daisies at the dead end of a dirt road. Two modular buildings serve as headquarters and the stable manager's home, and pole corrals house up to twenty horses and ponies. It is flanked by a low building that, according to legend, once served as General Patton's mess hall and is now a plumbing service. From there, it's just desert stretching northeast toward the San Bernardino Mountains.

In the shade of his stall, Cimi chews and licks thoughtfully. He is a tall, glossy bay with shapely haunches and shoulders and a deep chest, indisputably a Thoroughbred of fine pedigree and imperturbable poise.

"Cimi has so much faith in us because he was on the ground for twelve days; he couldn't fend for himself," says Virginia Davis, Pegasus stable manager, readying him for the day's work. "This horse is unflappable: wheelchairs bump him, people with walkers or canes are around, and he doesn't spook. He was disabled himself, and now he gives back to disabled people."

A middle-aged Brunhilda of the riding ring in huge tortoiseshell glasses, blonde bun, immaculate tan breeches, and tall black riding boots, Lori Sarner is president of Pegasus as well as its head instructor. She greets the volunteers who groom and saddle the horses and ready them for the morning's riders. Today the volunteers include Pete Petersen, Penny Carpenter, and Lee Sherman, all fit senior citizens from surrounding suburbs.

The horses are kept cool in their stalls by a misting system that automatically sprays cool water into the air when the temperature hits ninety degrees. Because the desert heat can reach as high as 130 degrees in the summer, they work only November through April. Their job is giving thirty- to forty-minute rides to handicapped adults and kids, reviving their bodies and their spirits.

And soon the riders roll in. In addition to a legless man in a wheelchair (a former highway patrol officer hit by a drunk driver), there are a dozen retarded children and brain-injured adults sipping drinks and eating snacks while talking in a shady ringside pavilion. Each rider wears a helmet and is attended by a helper on foot on each side, while another assistant leads the horse. One of the first eager riders is René Myers, who rolls her wheelchair up a loading ramp that brings her level with the horse's back. Cimi is led into the slot between the ramps, and with a boost from Pete, René settles onto the saddle. René was thrown from a car when she was eleven and suffered a brain injury. She used to show quarter horses as a girl and now, at thirty, she retains something of a rider's posture and ease, her long legs falling naturally into the proper heels-down position.

The Pegasus arena holds traffic cones, a low basketball hoop, and a soccer ball. With riders and attendants at the ready, Lori strides into the center of the ring and gives the command, "Walk on!"

Another rider, Bernie, clutches a pommel strap with his left hand; his right hand is a claw, his ankles turn in, and his toes are pointed and rigid. Penny, Pete, Lee, and other volunteers lead the horses forward. "Hahaha!" Bernie yells to the desert morning, his face flushed with joy. "Yahoo! Yahoooo!" Over Bernie's raw, crowing laughter, Lori says to us, "He's our hooray Henry."

"Okay, do a floppy doll with your right hand!" says Lori, and those who can, shake their hands. "Now take a deep breath and blow it out," she calls to the circling riders. "And now a whirligig; move the fingers on your affected hand," she says. "And look through the horse's ears! Up up up with the chin. Now close your eyes," she orders.

"With your left hand, do turkey wings, and everybody say gobble, gobble, gobble. Okay, now put your right hand on your shoulder."

After a few turns around the ring, René mops her face with her good left hand. At Lori's command to bow, riders bend forward as much as they can.

When René bows, her dark hair falls and melds into Cimi's mane, and her face rests on his neck in a combination of happy exhaustion and affection.

The mounted games work both sides of the body, limber the muscles, encourage better breathing, and improve balance. And they are just plain fun, as when the riders shoot hoops on horseback. With their assistants at their sides, René, Bernie, and the others ride purposefully up to the hoop and launch a soccer ball through the ring without pausing.

By the time Lori commands, "Go ho ho ho way down deep in your throat like Santa Claus," there are already smiles on every face. "This is not a pony ride—the horse is an apparatus for a mild form of physical therapy," says Lori. "Put a person on a horse, and they think and use motor skills. They literally get a mental lift."

In the 1980s, when Lori and her husband were living in London, she volunteered to help at a stable behind Buckingham Palace that featured a riding program for the disabled. At that time, she says, there were more than nine hundred riding-therapy chapters throughout Britain and Northern Ireland helping handicapped children.

When the Sarners moved to Palm Springs, California, she found a tiny bankrupt stable and launched Pegasus with one old pony named Patches. Cimmaron was the first donated horse. "I got into this because my mother was partially crippled with rheumatoid arthritis and deaf," Lori says. "These people are people, too, and one of the things I can give them because I love and know horses is exercise from the horse."

"Horses have always been our servants; they fought our battles, pulled our loads, hauled us around," she says. "In this century, we just use them for racing and pleasure, and we are losing them in every country in the world. They are expensive, not easy to keep, they take a lot of land, and that's becoming a scarcity in this country. We've made the horse a pouf, just a show horse. Take away the work ethic from a horse, and you take away a large part of his being. If we put them to work again, they will have real value. My point is to educate people that the horse can heal as well as pull loads and fight battles and go to war."

Cimmaron, an injured Thoroughbred racehorse, will never race but has found a career at Pegasus Riding Academy near Palm Springs, California.

The Pegasus horses include former polo ponies retired because of injury; a champion show jumper with one blind eye; a two-thousand-pound, one-time logging horse; and a retired Welsh show pony that was once purchased for a child competitor for ten thousand dollars.

Riders have favorites, and so do the horses: a girl named Debbie only rides Cimmaron, and when she dismounts, he moves his head over for a hug and kiss. Love and physical exercise are part of the healing equation, but every stroke patient who comes to Pegasus has experienced depression. And for men in particular, a horse bolsters their flagging macho, Lori explains.

"Here they are all John Wayne," says Lori, whose husband suffers from Parkinson's disease. "If they can do exercise and therapy on a horse, it's more fun and something they consider manly and out of doors. They take to this therapy and work hard, and we make it a bit competitive. Most cannot raise their affected arm, and their leg is partly paralyzed, and when they ride with other stroke patients who can get an arm up, they think, 'I want to do what he's doing!' Because we ride as a group, they see what other people have done. In a clinical environment alone with a therapist, they don't get this opportunity."

Medical training schools are recognizing the emotional and physical therapeutic values of riding, and often nursing students from the College of the Desert or the University of California at Riverside take part in Pegasus classes.

"People who have suffered a stroke had a life before it, and they have had a good life, and when a stroke hits them, they are reduced to nothing," says Lori. "We make them use both hands, and to get three baskets in a row is a very big deal! Then when their friends talk about their golf game or tennis, they can say, 'Hey, I rode a horse today.' They feel like a person again."

In the sunlight of the ring, Cimmaron walks steadily, rhythmically. René's neck, hips, and legs move in concert with the horse's neck, back, and ribs. For those who can't walk, the motions of riding are the closest thing in nature to the motion of a walking human.

Not everyone takes to riding immediately or voluntarily: a dark-haired autistic boy on a smaller horse is screaming, "I want to get off!" his nose running, his face wet with angry tears. Lori has seen this before and is unperturbed. "I have a credo: God has no stepchildren. That's the foundation of Pegasus," Lori says. "We have to be here for those who are difficult. It's easy to love the lovable, not so easy with the very difficult, the handful, but they need us most."

One reluctant rider had suffered from ovarian cancer and a stroke. She was undernourished, depressed, and passive. "At first, all she did was sit and cry," Lori recalls. "We put her in the saddle, and she rode around on the horse crying; we didn't care. After she rode for six weeks, she got well enough to fill out applications and get into assisted living for low-income people instead of being shifted around to friends. Riding helped her focus, she gained weight, and her whole life started to take shape."

"Depression is a big part of disability, and riding lifts people's spirits," says Lori. "Here it's what they *can* do that counts."

12

NOT WITHOUT MY SON

ELTON ACKERS AND HIS DOG, PEEWEE

FIVE DAYS AFTER Hurricane Katrina, the streets of New Orleans ran glassy with an evil gumbo of toxic chemicals, swollen corpses, live electric lines, uprooted giant oaks and magnolias, shattered glass, drowned cars, and rotting food. The Big Easy had finally taken the big hit, and up and down the coasts of Louisiana and Mississippi, especially in the Mississippi Delta soup bowl that circles New Orleans, people and animals were missing.

And Elton and Geneva Ackers had had enough. They sat on the steps of the New Orleans Convention Center in the stench and heat with thousands of other hungry and terrified people. "My baby say to me, 'Honey, I'm hungry,'" says Elton. "And I worried about my dog."

"I went upstairs, and they had dead bodies where they keep the meat," Elton recalls. "A baby, a white woman, and a black man died on a table right in front of me and my wife. There wasn't no doctors. The chief of police come with the National Guard, and he told us a lie. He say the water goin' down. And he say they gonna bring us food, but most people too sick to eat."

"And she say, 'Oh, baby, we not staying inside here.' I tell her I goin' home to get some food and come back with my dog," Elton tells us. At 5:00 a.m. on Friday, armed only with a flashlight, Elton started down Magazine Street, wading and climbing over debris and traveling three miles to their home on Robert Street, where he had left his dog, PeeWee, with Mac, a friend's pug, for company.

"Some parts, the water rise high; some parts, the water rise low," he says. Near home, the "water comin' up to here," he says, indicating his chest.

Like thousands of other residents, Elton and Geneva had waited too long to get out of town. The rain tore down and a tree smashed through their roof, but the wind was so strong they couldn't hear it fall. When the water rolled up the street and into their house, they set up a barbecue on a neighbor's porch, and camped there, stranded. I asked Elton why they hadn't left sooner.

"In Betsy [Hurricane Betsy in 1985] the water didn't take and come up as high as this," he explains. "We look at the water risin', and we never had nothing like that before. We had a portable TV, and it say the water gon' rise nine feet more, but then we couldn't start the car—the water take and kill all the 'lectric. So we say we just gon' sit here till somebody come get us."

Finally they climbed into a rescue boat, leaving food and water for the two dogs, expecting to be home in a day or two at most. The boat driver refused to take PeeWee and Mac.

As the days passed in the convention center, Elton worried about PeeWee every minute. And when he couldn't stand it any longer, he took action. When he opened his front door, the dogs greeted him with desperate eagerness. Storm water had saturated the furniture and floors of the shotgunstyle bungalow. But the gas was still on, and Elton boiled some eggs, made tuna salad from canned tuna, and fed himself and the dogs, and he dug out

Hurricane Katrina survivors Elton Ackers and his dog, PeeWee, in a ruined home in New Orleans. Thousands of pets left behind died, but Elton went back for PeeWee.

a change of clothes for himself and Geneva. Then he bagged up additional food and water and hiked back through the water to the center. It was about noon on the first of a month of ninety-degree rainless days that followed the hurricane.

At the center, Elton left the supplies with Geneva. Then he headed home again.

"I tell her they three buses left, and they gon' make you get on the buses, but I ain't goin'," he explains. "I worried 'bout my dog."

On Sunday, as Elton sat with PeeWee and Mac, a helicopter whirled above their house, shearing off the few shingles that had not been blown away by the hurricane or skinned off by the fallen tree. "The roof wide open on account of the tree, and the man say we send you a boat, you got to get in," Elton says. "And I say no, I'm not gon' get on it this time. Not without my son."

Now, six months after the hurricane, it is ten in the morning, and the old men on Robert Street are at their positions holding down various porches on the block. They sit on the verandah at Gladys's house next-door to Elton's bungalow and on the stoop at Roland's across the street. They do not sit indoors on the new ivory faux suede sofas bought with insurance money, a short one for PeeWee and a longer one for Elton and Geneva. They lounge outdoors with their beer cans, surveying the variegated philodendrons twining up porch pillars, the jasmine blooming again on the chain-link fences, the hedges and trees struggling to revive from a salt water soaking, and the piles of mattresses, plaster, tires, and mildewed furniture heaped at the curb. They watch Mexican roofing crews remove blue tarps and reshingle roofs.

Geneva, who works as a cashier at a local Walgreens, is gone for the day. Elton, retired from construction jobs at oil plants, is home with PeeWee, tracking the neighborhood news, which is shouted across the street.

"What's happenin', Ed?"

"Hey Duke-Duke!"

"Hey, alright, how ya'll feelin'?"

"You goin' to the parade?" someone asks Elton.

"Ain't getting in no crowds," says Elton. "Where he gone today?"

"He went fishin'. See what he come back with. I tol' him you catch 'em and I cook 'em."

Elton at sixty-three is lean and fine-featured with bright, even teeth and piercing hazel-gold eyes set against glossy black skin. PeeWee at seven years old is also compact, a moist, rich chocolate-cake black with undertones of dun on his legs.

"When he born, he was tan," says Elton, offering us baby pictures of his puppy, black with tan points, cuddled up to a plush toy chimpanzee. PeeWee tolerates us, but his gaze and his considerable ears are always fixed on Elton with the fierce quiet of a professional bodyguard. He is Elton's security system in more ways than one. "I bring him to church in the car and leave the glass down but don't worry 'bout nobody get in the car," Elton says, proud of his friend, his four-legged son.

PeeWee is the thirteenth puppy of Princess, Elton's late Belgian shepherd bitch, and Chico, a local black Labrador. He was born in the backyard of this cozy rented cottage, and because he was the smallest, Geneva named him PeeWee.

The houses here on Robert Street and in every parish for miles around are marked with the graffiti of loss: spray-painted x's with a code from rescue workers noting the date they looked into the property and what they found. Just as often there are messages painted by the residents: "Outside cat, no bird" or "Two dogs, outdoor cat."

We have showed up in time for lunch, and Elton feeds us hot pork ribs and red beans and rice and violently red hot dogs slathered with relish. "You got enough meat in there?" he fusses over our portions. "You want you another beer?" He has been working on cold cans of beer all morning, and Judy and I each accept one with lunch just to be sociable. PeeWee watches us, his chin on his paws, from his ivory sofa.

"Daddy comin'," Elton says, his gold eyes catching PeeWee's lighter gold ones. "What my boy say? My son say he ain't hungry."

The beer early in the day (for us) hits Judy hardest. Soon after lunch, she is nodding off on the other sofa. "You lay down and take you a nap and look at television," Elton advises, cracking open another can and heading to the kitchen to wash dishes.

So we join PeeWee and watch the post-hurricane Mardi Gras that is unrolling just blocks away: the Boeuf Gras float glides down Canal Street, steam rising from a giant bull's nostrils, wafting through his exaggerated eyelashes and an outsized garland of flowers on his neck. Brass marching bands strut through streets littered ankle deep with Mardi Gras coins, colored beads, and trash. People stagger, whoop and bellow, some carrying tall glasses of rum and fruit juice, a concoction called a Hurricane. The noise and color of the parade is flanked by block after block of dark and silent office buildings pitifully armored in plywood.

Around us, however, things are tranquil. The walls of Elton and Geneva's living room display portraits of Martin Luther King Jr. and a Jesus with a bleeding, radiant heart. Dozens of family photos are propped on the mantels of the four fireplaces, one in every room but the kitchen.

"I got three daughters, they live in Thibodeaux. I got no son; PeeWee my son," Elton tells us. "I talk to PeeWee more than I talk to people. It works out."

When Elton was hospitalized for nearly a week following a stroke a few years ago, PeeWee refused to eat. From the hospital, Elton asked Geneva at home to put the phone to the dog's ear. "I tell him, 'I am comin' home, baby! Daddy comin' to see his son. You got to eat your food.'"

PeeWee did. A few days later, Elton arrived home to an ecstatic dog that licked his face. And life went on smoothly in the bungalow on Robert Street. And then came Katrina.

When the boat driver agreed to let the dogs in his boat, Elton, PeeWee, and Mac got aboard. That led to rides together in a truck, a helicopter, a plane to Atlanta, and a bus to Eaton, Georgia, where housing was available for the hurricane evacuees. Since Mac's owner didn't want him back, Elton gave Mac to a friend there. PeeWee never left Elton's side. And they both missed Geneva.

"PeeWee wag his tail every time a heavyset woman come by—he miss her too," says Elton. Three weeks later, they rejoined Geneva, who was staying with family in Jackson, Mississippi.

The three returned home just before Christmas to a bungalow with a new roof. They bought new furniture and appliances, and Elton refinished the dining-room table and chairs and the wide planks of the wooden floor.

Today the music of Robert Street is black laughter and mourning doves and car horns honking. Sometimes Elton and his friends turn on a car stereo and leave the windows rolled down to share it. Far away there is a distant hyena howl of police sirens, as cops deal with drunks along the Mardi Gras parade routes. New Orleans is making a big show of being brave. A pink, yellow, and green billboard along the nearby highway declares: "Nothing cancels Mardi Gras. NOTHING."

"Don't look on the other side of Canal Street; it bring tears to your eyes," Elton warns us, but that is just what we want to see, a place where many people did not or could not leave, and where many pets were left behind to the mercy of the fast-rising brown water.

So we pile into our rental car, Elton in front with me driving, PeeWee's head between us, his torso and tail with Judy and the cameras in the backseat. From parish to parish, there are few street signs left standing and fewer working stoplights, but Elton navigates us around the sporadic street parties of Mardi Gras to the lower ninth ward. Everywhere signs are tacked to utility poles advertising for subcontractors, mold treatment, tree care and removal, or workers wanted.

When Elton gets out of the car, PeeWee gives an anxious gasp that turns to a whine until we let him out too. "Come on, son!" Elton calls. Then he trots after Elton, his tail waving happily, padding through clover that rises green through miles of wreckage.

New Orleans's lower-ninth ward looks as if it has been mashed flat by a divine fist. The further east we walk, the more crumpled and splintered it becomes: cars tossed into trees and flattened; chain-link fencing whipped into snarls; beams, chairs, tables, and bedding crushed—an apocalyptic mess. Where fragments of houses still stand, doors loom ajar in a birdless silence. A few Red Cross and FEMA business cards blow across floors deep in dried, curling muck, the residue of the river.

"My sister lived here," says Elton. "She had a little-bitty, expensive-ass dog she pay $1,000 for, but when the boat come and they tell her she cain't take it, she leave it here. It woulda fit in her pocket, but she left it, and it gone."

"Nobody live here now. They scared to come back. Imagine how many people not in they house—it make you sick just lookin' at it," says Elton. "They cain't come back, they cain't put nothin' here. Gon' be under the water sooner or later. That gon' be our river."

"My mama, she lost her house too," he adds. "She don't smoke, drink, or cuss, and she don't never wear pantses. First time I see her wear pantses was to get in that helicopter."

We make our way back to the car and to Elton's house through jesters and courtesans, warriors and nymphs, bagpipers playing "When the Saints Go Marching In," and trios of velvet-caped riders on horseback with slit-eyed masks. Saddened by the blasted city, we ask Elton fewer questions, but PeeWee has had a good walk with his best friend. He assumes his perch: quiet, cheerful, and alert.

"I love dogs 'cause they can't help theyself," says Elton, who was unique in that aspect in his large family. "Mama had nine children, and I am the only one love dogs the way I do, any kind of dog 'long as I had a dog. She didn't 'low no dogs in the house so I'd wait 'til Mama go to sleep, then I put the dog in bed with me. I caught plenty whipping for dogs. When I was eight, I had me a Belgian shepherd. Me and the dog could take and be with each other, and he wouldn't tell Mama if I done bad things."

"The last one I had when I was living with Mama was a cocker spaniel named Black Gal. She was blind, but she get in trucks better than you could, and you can see."

Not all his neighbors treat their dogs well, Elton confides to us. There are men who beat them, who drag them behind cars, who kill their dogs trying to rule them. There are those who train dogs to fight.

"I tell 'em, man, you ain't got to holler at your dog. I don't want my dog to be scared of me. If I see somebody mistreat they dog, I'm getting in the humbug with them. I have to. It seem like it hurt me when they take and misuse they dog."

"You talk to a dog like you talkin' to children," he advises, and we see he practices this with PeeWee.

"I just an animal freak; I love every dog; I love animals, period!" Elton says. "When I was comin' up, I used to clean the stables on North Rampart, take care of they horses and mules after school in the evenin'. They was sightseeing horses for the carriages. Once I was bringin' 'em to get shoes on, and the horse bucked me off on St. Claude Street in front of a bus!" And he laughs at the memory.

"I love my wife and the ground my wife walk on," he says with warmth. "I got a big wife, and I got a big bed. PeeWee take and jump up with us in bed ever' night, and he fall asleep watchin' television with us too."

Surviving Katrina reinforced what matters to Elton. "In this neighborhood, when we gone after the hurricane, some of my so-called friends took stuff out my house—they figure we not comin' back. And then they have the nerve to send us a weddin' invitation. But it don't matter. My mama livin', my sisters and my brother, my wife. We got our dog, and we got our life."

"He adores you, doesn't he, Elton?" I ask.

"I live to adore him too," says Elton. "And I ain't gon' leave him again."

Sign in East St. Louis, Missouri, where dogfighting is an epidemic. Randy Grim works this neighborhood, saving dogs from death from fighting or being used as pit-bull bait.

SWEETNESS IN THE MEAN STREETS

RANDY GRIM, HIS DOG QUENTIN,
AND STRAY RESCUE OF ST. LOUIS

WE WERE JOUNCING along the potholed, curbless tracks that pass for roads in East St. Louis scouting for Randy Grim's "kids"—feral and abandoned dogs. A jerry-rigged capture net swung from the ceiling of Randy's silver jeep, loose dog kibble rattled in the rear compartment, and Randy's canine best buddy, Quentin, riding in front between Randy and me, kept skidding off the console into my lap, his claws failing to find traction as we turned corners or bashed into ruts.

Around us was a scene from a war zone: burnt roofs of bungalows collapsed inward, lawns given over to mattresses, garbage, clothes, and beer and whiskey bottles. Trees punched up through roofs and splayed through glassless windows; alleys so choked with brush they were no longer navigable; and discarded sofas and chairs littering the yards and empty lots. Against all surrounding evidence, several faded, hand-stenciled signs nailed to cottonwood trees declared JESUS LOVE YOU [*sic*].

Except for the fact that there were no cars upside down in trees, this urban neighborhood looked very much like the ninth ward of New Orleans we saw after Hurricane Katrina.

"There's one! There's one of my kids," says Randy, pulling the jeep to the edge of a vacant lot thick with scrubby box elder and mulberry trees. "Here, honey, come on baby girl," Randy calls as he walks toward the corner, where a golden dog lies curled in the chill winter sunlight. Circular depressions in the grass mark the spots where Randy's "boys and girls" sleep and sun themselves and wait for him to bring them meals. Armed with a can of hot dogs and some beef jerky—"junk food, but they like it"—Randy moves quietly toward the dog.

At first, we do not smell her, but as we get closer we can see her black muzzle is frozen in a teeth-baring agonized grimace, and her left hind leg is broken, angled back and upward at the hock.

"She was pregnant, and she died in pain here," says Randy, sitting on his heels close to the dog. "I am so sorry, honey." He whispers a benediction over the body before returning to the jeep.

Randy is the founder of Stray Rescue of St. Louis, an organization that attempts to reclaim the strays of South City and East St. Louis. He is broad-shouldered, tall, and in his mid-forties with gentle eyes, fine tan skin, and graying ash-blonde hair. Under a heavy winter coat and a sweater, his right shoulder bears a color tattoo of his beloved Charlie, a rescued but not exactly wholly-rehabilitated pit bull, and his left shoulder displays the Chinese character for dog.

He describes himself as a "recluse until I have a martini in me," and he is not exaggerating, but Quentin and a cause have helped him overcome that. Working the wasteland of East St. Louis with Randy, we see more dogs than people—only the occasional man or boy on foot in the crumbled silent road. Incredibly, some of the single-storey brick bungalows are occupied. They sit behind wrought-iron security doors, and there are dead cars and vans collapsed on flat tires inside padlocked, chain-link fences like wagons encircling the house for additional protection.

We spot one woman picking up trash in the ditch around her mailbox as two dogs scamper across her small, unfenced yard.

"Are those your dogs?" Randy calls to her.

"No, they ain't mine," she says. "They don't belong to nobody."

And that is the problem in the mean streets of East St. Louis. Dogs are born here; dogs are dumped here. (Randy rescued one with a microchip showing it had been adopted at a shelter on the other side of the Mississippi River.) Dogs are forced to fight and get shot and maimed here. But today, Randy's usual hungry canine characters are largely missing.

"This is freakin' me out," he worries. "The last few days I've been looking for them and it's gone, gone, gone—the only dogs I found are mutilated. Oh—here's Daddy's girl!"

Out of the weeds slinks a young tricolor bitch, hopeful, frightened, and lured by the aroma of the hot dogs. She licks her lips and tucks her tail, squatting submissively in the middle of the road, and Randy squats, too, and tosses her treats. Soon she is joined by a black male, limping, with hackles raised. He is more wary and runs wide of Randy, declining the snacks. The dogs are right to be distrustful.

"More than half the dogs we rescue have gunshot wounds," says Randy, who has been shot at twice himself here. "And in that house right there," pointing out a green house with yellow trim, "they fight dogs. We took one out of there; they had sliced him up to use as bait for the pit bulls. I think he's gonna survive, but he may lose a leg."

We circle around Galilee Central Church and Nelson Mandela School, up and down streets, until we pass a sign: "Pit Bull Puppies for Sale." A black-and-white pit bull barks furiously at us from a short chain tangled even shorter in scrubby trees, while a second dog is chained to a box in the middle of a puddle.

"Oh, good, like we need more pit bulls," says Randy, who pops out to check on the condition of the chained dogs. It's not just curiosity—he has been known to steal starving or abused pets. As we start to drive on, a car pulls up to ours.

"You feedin' them mutts?" asks the driver, a man with cornrows, outsized diamond stud earrings, and four gold teeth.

"Yes, I'm from Stray Rescue, and we work here trying to get the dogs off the streets," says Randy.

"You ain't helpin'," says the man. "We ain't got no choice but to shoot 'em—they all in the trash cans," the man says and pulls away.

"Well, maybe if you *fed* them they wouldn't have to *eat garbage*," hisses Randy, once we are out of earshot. "If you are blaming the decline in property values around here on stray dogs, you need to wake up. And may you die a horrible, slow death too!"

Quentin has been silent throughout the search, tensely scanning through the windshield for the hungry dogs, whimpering only when Randy leaves the jeep. He is golden sorrel with gold eyes, pale toenails, and enormous bat-like expressive ears, broad through the jowls, with a tail curled happily over his back, a slight hump in his nose, and a tongue speckled with black, possibly the legacy of basenji and pit bull. Topaz yellow rhinestones on Quentin's collar spell "Cha Cha Dog," a gift from a friend when Randy performed on *Dancing with the Stars*. (Dogs and dance are the two things that can draw him out of seclusion.)

"Quentin is the smartest dog I've met in my life," says Randy, who calls the dignified dog "Daddy's angel muffin" or "Quent-a-lot," among other endearments.

"It took awhile to bond with him, because it gave me the creeps at first, how smart he is. He opens the fridge with his mouth and says 'come on' to my other dogs. [Randy's house holds a pack of eight.] I am not religious, but I believe in something higher than all of us, and he and I were meant to be together and make a difference. Together we are able to kick butt."

The butt Randy and Quentin kick is antiquated municipal policies about animal welfare, and euthanasia nationwide. It's vital to do euthanasia right—to do it with speed, kindness, and minimal pain. And Quentin gives this cause "street cred" because, unlike any other known dog, he survived the gas chamber.

Quentin came to Randy after his former owners surrendered him to the St. Louis Animal Regulation Center and requested that he be euthanized.

Randy Grim has helped save more than 5,000 dogs from starvation and neglect. He will take these puppies—found in East St. Louis—to his clinic for care and eventual adoption.

Their reason for wanting to kill the emaciated year-old dog? "We are moving to an apartment." Quentin was placed in the gas chamber with other unwanted dogs. After the regulation thirty minutes, the doors were opened. Quentin was standing on a pile of canine corpses, growling and wagging his tail.

"I don't believe in too many miracles because there's so much sad in the world, but the vets don't know why he survived," says Randy. "And if the chamber leaked, why did all the other dogs die?"

Randy was already a lifetime animal rescuer, and Quentin became his best friend and ally in the effort, venturing daily into streets that are bad urban legend. "I am socially phobic, afraid of germs from people but not dogs," Randy confesses. "I take Paxil and when it gets bad, go to Xanax, but I'm never afraid here. The only time I feel at peace is here, because I feel real purpose."

Randy was born in Verdun, France, the middle of five children, and raised in Washington, D.C. His late father, an Army colonel, "was a jerk," Randy says. "The only time there was harmony in our house was when there was a stray," he remembers. "So I would steal a can of tuna and go sit by the sewer and feed stray cats; I could empathize with them. Our first dog was Rebel, an Irish setter. I was five, and my brother and I found him, bone thin, in the snow and saw the pain in his eyes. I connected with him on a level I don't think five-year-olds are meant to. It was my first lesson in empathy. After that we always had four or five dogs at our house. It was the only time our father was normal."

"I majored in phys ed to please my dad, but I hated kids and didn't want to teach it," he says. "So then I became the worst flight attendant in the world—I worked for Eastern, TWA, and Ozark. I did it for the travel, but what I really did was pick up strays in other countries and smuggle them home in the airplane restroom. If you were ever flying and wondered why the restroom was always in use, that was me. But I didn't want to make a career of asking people, 'Do you want chicken or beef?' all my f—g life."

And he hasn't: since founding Stray Rescue in 1998, Randy has helped redeem more than five thousand dogs as well as hundreds of cats from starvation and neglect on the streets of the city. At any given time, there are 150 to 300 rescued cats and dogs in Stray Rescue foster homes, and he and his three hundred volunteers manage to rescue one to two thousand dogs each year.

"Quentin did more for me than a therapist did in fifteen years," says Randy, who has written about Quentin in *Miracle Dog: How Quentin Survived the Gas Chamber to Speak for Animals on Death Row*. "We are a match made in heaven. We are supposed to work together, to do good things for animals. Either that or I can let my phobias and anxieties keep me staying in a box. That's why God created pills—and dogs."

Randy drives onto a corner, where a man, swigging from a bottle in a paper bag, shuffles through the back door of his home as a golden, short-haired female and a longer-haired black male dog bounce up to greet Randy. Randy has supplied the two primitive doghouses on the unfenced yard, which is junk free and neatly mowed, and these two strays come and go as they please, showing up for their daily feeding.

"Where's my Charlie? There's my girl!" he says, patting them and feeding them treats. "Honey, hang in there. I'll be back for you."

And he will. This pair (Randy refers to them as a married couple and vows he will see them adopted together) is trusting enough to allow him to handle them. And soon—once there is room at the vet, with one of his foster families, or at the shelter—they will get off the streets. They have a chance at successful adoption, but that's not true of all his cats and dogs.

"People say we are 'no kill' but I hate the term 'no kill,'" he says emphatically, blowing cigarette smoke out of the jeep's window. "What do you do with unadoptable dogs? And how many Randys are there? We put down five to ten a year, and what we do is responsible kill."

Randy estimates there are forty thousand stray dogs in St. Louis alone. That's not uncommon for big cities, he believes, and it's most common where there's urban decay.

"In this neighborhood, you don't even see police; there's no vets here, nothing to help the animals," he rails. "We are the only non-third-world country with this problem. The 'rules' say I'm only supposed to handle adoptable animals. How do we make it politically correct to care about these guys? Why are they second-class citizens?"

Off Forest Street, Randy parks the jeep and enters a yard strewn with ruptured plastic bags of garbage, from which a cordial young black-and-white dog is trying to make a meal. In the overgrown jumble marked with homemade crucifixes, plywood gnomes, and peeling wooden Santas, he finds four roly-poly puppies cuddling for warmth on a piece of foam rubber in the brush. Randy judges they are seven to eight weeks old, mature enough to leave their mother, and scoops them up. He scavenges a red plastic milk crate from the junk, and the four pups—three black and one chocolate brown, probably pit-bull mixes—go into the crate, which I hold on my lap. After one or two dignified sniffs, Quentin ignores them, and the puppies, complaining in tiny squeaky groans, swiftly fall asleep in a pile.

Dark is coming—no time for us to be on the East Side—and we need to get the puppies to the clinic, so we drive back to the city. "When I die, just filet me and throw me over on the East Side so the dogs can have some food," says Randy as the jeep barrels away from the melancholy land below the freeway exit.

We deliver the pups to Stray Rescue headquarters in the Lafayette Square neighborhood. A vivid and cheerful Charles Houska animal mural brightens the parking-lot wall, and framed Houska prints are on display around the lobby of the single-storey modern building. The facility has five full-time staff, and Randy serves as director and fund-raiser, as well as keeper of the group's spokesdog.

Handing the puppies over to the enthusiastic women behind the reception counter, Randy leads us backstage to visit Hop, the dog that was used as pit-bull bait. Hop is a compact, golden-brown mixed breed, possibly Labrador and shepherd, with numerous shaved patches revealing fresh sutures on his side, chest, and legs. He puts no weight on his left front leg as he greets Randy with humble excitement.

"My booboodoo—I'm very proud of you," coos Randy, who squats in the narrow kennel to stroke the dog's shoulders and kiss the scarred forehead.

Hop looks up at him with meek and adoring eyes. "This is just the best—when they come to trust you, because on the street they are so wary."

Another population of rescued dogs waits for us at Randy's three-storey red-brick Victorian townhouse in the gentrifying neighborhood of Benton Park. The home faces a large tranquil park replete with ponds and sits just down a rise from the Anheuser-Busch brewery. We clump up steep stairs to the elegant hideaway, with high ceilings and doorway transoms and a dining-room table ornamented with a vase of stately calla lilies garnished with a red bandana. A hockey stick autographed by center Keith Tkachuk of the St. Louis Blues rests on an ottoman, and the bronze-and-gold walls display portraits of Quentin and some of Randy's previous dogs.

"Being gay doesn't automatically mean I love Judy Garland—I love ice hockey *and* ballroom dance," says Randy. "But who'd want to date me? I have eight dogs in my house. Are you guys sure it doesn't smell in here? Tell me the truth." We reassure him it doesn't smell the least bit doggy—and it doesn't.

Randy has sawed off the top half of the dining room door to the kitchen, and three or four blonde dog heads peer over the top of it. We look over it toward the kitchen at the far end of the floor and a shaggy black head peeks down the kitchen staircase—this is Horse, a deaf husky mix.

"Half my kids are ancient—they're fourteen to sixteen—and the others are two to seven years old, so I know half my family is gonna die in the next few years," says Randy.

I make the mistake of moving toward the pack, and there's a horrendous rush and boom as something hard and determined smacks the half-door, bellowing at me.

"Charlie! No! Sit!" Randy says in a commanding bass voice, interposing himself and shoving me back from the doorway. "Don't look at Charlie—that's him—and for God's sake don't try to touch him. The others are okay. I rescued Charlie from a fight ring; he wants to kill everyone. He's good with other dogs, and he's my sleeping buddy, but at the shelter he bit everyone and all the volunteers. He has to wear a wire muzzle like Hannibal Lecter when he goes anywhere."

In his "Zen room"—the palm-thick front parlor—the walls and fire-place mantel are painted bright gold, and there is a Moroccan-style hang-ing lamp framed by tent-like swags of tropical mosquito netting. In the center of the room, in a blue bowl poised on a hanging marble table, is a Siamese fighting fish named Pumpernickel, also rescued ("Kids were going to flush him down the toilet," Randy explains).

A teeny blonde mongrel not much bigger than a large caterpillar and sporting a blue-and-green pastel plaid coat scrabbles across the pine floors and leaps joyously at us, begging to be picked up, then slurps our chins, noses, and eyes. "Ichi!" Randy says, hugging the dog. "This little guy—Ichiban—was going to be euthanized at a shelter, and I was doing a book-signing there and smuggled him out under my coat. Something was wrong with his back knees, but after surgery, he could run like crazy."

"My favorite thing in the whole world is to lie in bed with my dogs and watch cartoons," he says. (Not quite: Randy takes ballroom dance lessons several times a week, and he and his dance partner won jive and cha-cha at the national ballroom dance competition.)

Randy's least favorite thing are germs (he was convinced he had the plague, anthrax, and bird flu, among others) and being with unfamiliar humans. Despite those very real phobias, he travels often to promote humane practices—lately to North Carolina, New Mexico, Georgia, Kansas, and Oklahoma—with Quentin serving as the news peg for meet-ings and the photo op for media. Randy says the two of them have per-suaded fifty communities to close gas chambers. Three states have banned them statewide, including, most recently, Illinois, where Quentin and Randy appeared with the governor at the signing of the new regulation.

"Quentin taught me how to help more animals than I thought I could," says Randy, at ease among the pillows of his living-room sofa. "He really knows his job; he hopes it's gonna help other dogs."

"We recently went to a town in Georgia where the animal-control staff were very proud of their new gas chamber. They told me, 'We just stopped shooting them,'" he says. "In situations like that, I can't let how I really feel take over. So I thought, Randy, you have to act! Show them they can be progressive, make their town look good, get some good news in the press about them. I talked to them with no judgment, and Quentin does his job."

Tomorrow morning, Randy and Quentin will mount a rescue expedition back to East St. Louis. Tonight he is with his rescued pack: Quentin in his arms, Ichi washing his ears, and Charlie and crew panting behind the sawed-off door.

"I'm only one person working for animals," Randy says. "I'm no hero; this is not a job; it's what I am."

Jack and Bob spend part of the year in Indio, California, and part in Montana, but they are always together.

14

DOG IS MY CO-PILOT

BOB BRADLEY AND HIS DOG, JACK

IT'S NOT THE 1966 Jaguar XKE in which Bob Bradley is driving twenty miles an hour over the speed limit. It's not his fleet of polo ponies—bay and black, taut and fit, purchased in New Zealand, Mexico, and Argentina.

It's Bob himself, who is wiry with thick silver hair, bright blue eyes, and a smattering of movie-star glamour. He's the kind of man who, even in his sixties, provokes gorgeous young women to lean out of their pickup-truck windows and purr, "Hi, honey, you're lookin' sharp," and mean it.

And there are plenty of pretty women and gorgeous horses in Bob's winter habitat, the El Dorado Polo Club, part of the vast, irrigated green fields in the Coachella Valley in the California desert near Indio. Bob is one of twenty-one partners who keep their polo ponies in these hundred and seventy lush, flat acres framed in white fences and high hedges of pink oleander.

Around the edge of the polo fields, a series of single-storey brick buildings contain box stalls of fine, lean horses with shaved manes above slim necks and restless bodies. Bob's office—at one end of his stable—features a shower and dressing area and is tasteful in a sporting club way. It is part utilitarian and part shrine to the high-spirited times that come with the sport.

Somebody gave him a life-sized cardboard cutout of a bikinied model, and a ten-foot python skin spans one wall above photographs of Bob with Hillary Clinton; of shirtless Argentinean polo players doing the limbo under a hitching rail ("when those Argentineans get liquor in 'em, they take their clothes off," says Bob chuckling); of Bob and famed natural-horsemanship trainer Buck Brannaman. "I know Buck," says Bob. "His stuff works if you have one or two cow horses. When you have eighteen horses giving you shit, it doesn't. You don't take the time you need to take."

Polo is like bumper cars at high speed without seatbelts. Riders gallop half a dozen horses into a lather over six time periods called chukkers. It's a matter of certainty that the players will be injured, and Bob has played for more than thirty years. "Let's see, yeah, I broke a couple of ribs with horses going over," he recalls. "I fell on my own hand. I broke collar bones, got forty stitches in the back of my head from hooves . . ." Bob is genuinely cool about the battering he takes. All of this is de rigueur for a speedy equestrian sport.

As a retired, successful corporate CEO, Bob could do anything he likes. What he likes is polo, he says, for the down-to-earth people, for the outdoor life, and for the creatures.

When he was a boy, Bob wanted to be a doctor—he opened an office in an Allied moving box when he was about ten. Ultimately, though, he went into business. He and his father, Lee, a mechanical engineer, started a company in St. Paul, Minnesota, manufacturing metal component parts for agricultural, automotive, and aircraft use—everything from cribbage boards to diesel engines. Bob sold the company for tens of millions in 1997. Along the way, he started playing polo on Sundays in Maple Plain, Minnesota, and then in California. There followed a divorce from his first wife, and a marriage to a much younger woman who also played polo. And not long after that, Bob found himself on the receiving end of heartbreak from his second wife.

"My heart said she's the rest of my life," he says. "It became a fight between my brain and my heart, and the brain said, 'Get out,' and the heart said, 'Ah, give it another chance.' It's the same damn thing; the heart over-rules the brain for awhile. Love is a risky thing, while business is a calculated risk. The worst is that pain in the stomach. That lasts for a long time."

So there was a second divorce. And then he was alone in his various par-adises, at least for the time being. But not quite. Bob met a puppy, the last of a litter of five offspring of an Australian shepherd and blue-heeler bitch crossed with a Catahoula dog father. "Jack was the last of the litter; nobody wanted him," says Bob. "He talked me into it."

From the floor of his office in the polo barn today, sturdy, bobtailed Jack gazes up adoringly at Bob, the flicker of banked fun in his watchful eyes along with a spooky-deep intelligence.

"Jack has become the best dog I ever had, my best friend and companion," says Bob, who has a good-sized population of past dogs to compare him with, among them Drake, his German shepherd; Basil, a bassett hound; Bubba, a bloodhound; and Sarge, a black Labrador. Jackie is Bob's polo, trail, ranch, and cow dog, and something more. When Bob was in bed for three days recently with an exceptionally nasty flu, Jack sat beside the bed and watched him.

"Dogs don't have another agenda. He's a dog for a single person, more focused on me," says Bob. "But he'll ask to go out if things are boring, right, Jackie?" Jack mumble-growls like a man with his mouth full of sand-wich, shoots Bob a look, and does a shoulder roll across the toes of Bob's cowboy boots as if to say, "Look at me! Rub my stomach! Let's go! God, it's boring in here!"

So we get a move on, at Jack's insistence. The grass at each stable is golf-tee fine and verdant, the aisles neatly raked. Bob and Jack lead us down the shady stable aisle, making introductions: to a sorrel Mexican Thoroughbred named Bonbon; to Gato, an Argentine Thoroughbred; to Suave, an Argentine Thoroughbred mare with the distinctive South American Criollo blood that gives her speckled roan legs; and to a New Zealand Thoroughbred named Hanna.

"Some say mares have more heart," Bob explains. "I don't care whether it's a mare or a gelding, as long as they have four good legs and work well."

"Argentinean horses can be shy—training methods in America, New Zealand, and England are kinder, gentler," he explains, as some horses dodge our outstretched hands and hide their faces in the corners of the tile stalls. "Ministro, you old fart!" he greets one gelding, a black Argentinean horse with white stockings whose markings give him the appearance of wearing a clerical collar and cuffs.

When Bob moves toward the shed to get his golf cart, Jack bounds ahead, ready to ride shotgun. He knows his place, and it's in the passenger seat.

An orchestra of mynah birds sings among the pink and white roses on the stable patio beside a black Kenworth semitruck tractor trailer. Bob hauls his fifteen horses in this high and glossy rig. This is the last week of the winter season at the Palm Springs area polo clubs, and many ponies are already turned out in neighboring ranches on the spring grass, their lean ribs beginning to fatten in the off-season. Soon Bob and Jack and the horses will head for northwest Wyoming and his Hoback River ranch, where a cutthroat trout stream runs just out the front door of a log house built to order with old-fashioned elegance and a view of the Wyoming Range. He will make this drive, as he makes all his drives, with Jack in the co-pilot seat.

Bob may still have those stomach pains for his lost love, but he isn't saying much about that. He will say Jack saved his life in a way, that Jack takes care of him, that his leftover pup has stood by him. "More and more I realize how unusual Jack is," he says. "He is kind with dogs and people. There's a lot going on behind those brown eyes."

15

NO MATTER WHAT

SHANNON LARSON AND HER DOG MASON

When Mason smiles—and he always smiles—he grins all the way back to his ears, his outsized tongue lolls out like a pink hand towel, and his deep brown eyes shine. It's a mouth easily big enough to encircle Harley, his Lhasa apso pal, who at this moment is trying vainly to gain some purchase on Mason's back from the vantage point of a crushed velvet sofa so he can hump his way to doggie dominance. Mason is unperturbed. Very little bothers him: not the yipping, dancing Harley; not the chickens in a farmyard where he often plays; not assorted children thumping and pulling on him.

But once, a crucial once, he *was* perturbed; he got his way and it saved lives.

Mason belongs to Shannon Larson, a single mom in her mid-twenties whose round cheekbones, hairband, and bangs give her the appearance of a more serene Sally Field. Shannon lives in the tiny town of Banks in the Willamette Valley of Oregon about forty-five minutes from the coast. It's a moist, green paradise of sheep pastures, hazelnut orchards, and vegetable stands, where mammoth logging trucks hauling Douglas fir topped with

Mason saved his owner, Shannon Larson of Banks, Oregon, and other family pets from a fire in their rural Oregon home.

Chance and Hope, two Great Pyrenees dogs, were found starving in a ditch with shattered hind legs. Adopted by Don and Darlene Ahlstrom, today they work in a Rochester, Minnesota, long-term care home.

Lynne Warfel-Holt of Northfield, Minnesota, with her rescued horse, Twister, and rescued bassett hound, Francis. "Animals teach me everything about love, and especially they teach forgiveness and grace," Lynne says.

In the Maricopa County Jail in Phoenix, Arizona, female inmates learn to care for abandoned or seized animals such as this pit bull mix. Cats, dogs, birds, and ferrets are among the animals sheltered in the old jail, while prisoners live in a tent city in the desert.

Libby's job is to help with temperament testing on potentially adoptable dogs at the Willamette Humane Society in Salem, Oregon.

New Orleans resident Elton Ackers calls PeeWee his son and treats him like one.

Randy Grim cuddles Quentin, who somehow survived the gas chamber at the pound. Randy rescues feral dogs and cats from the streets of East St. Louis. The tattoo is a portrait of Charlie, a pit bull Randy took away from a dogfighting ring.

Jack the devoted cattle dog helped his owner, Bill Bradley, a polo player in Indio, California, survive a shattered romance.

Before her car accident, René Myers loved to ride horses. Now she is able to ride again on Cimmaron, who survived a gruesome injury in a trailer to become a therapy horse at Pegasus Riding Academy near Palm Springs, California.

"He's always been a best friend to me, more than people," says Shannon Larson of Banks, Oregon. "With Mason, I know somebody loves me no matter what."

"What do I do about the hole in my heart?" Dawsen asked his mother, Trina, when his parents divorced and his father left him and his brother. Nickey was the answer.

The women of The Other Elizabeth, a fine jewelry store in Millwood, Virginia, bring their rescued pets to work. Griselda, the onetime trailer-court cat, now belongs to store owner Elizabeth Locke and sports jewel-studded collars.

Hilleary Bogley works with animals from the hills and farms of Virginia, getting dogs off chains and away from starvation and drug dealers. "Animals are close to my heart; they give me everything," she says.

Annie had been battered by someone who cracked her nose, broke her jaw, and pulped her eye. When Pat Reever of Fairfax, Virginia, took her in, she was also pregnant with oversized puppies that had to be aborted. Now she is cheerful and eager to be petted.

Eileen McCarthy, founder of Midwest Avian Adoption & Rescue Services in St. Louis Park, Minnesota, with Angel, a rescued cockatoo.

Horse trainers Ron Danta and Danny Robertshaw of Camden, South Carolina, take in needy, injured, or abandoned cats and dogs and find them new owners. Since Hurricane Katrina, they have rescued more than eight hundred dogs. They also adopt many dogs from a local shelter and find new owners for them.

Ron and Danny arranged for Ebenezer, a wirehaired dachshund puppy-mill survivor, to be flown to them from Kentucky.

Lucy Warner Bruntjen at Ellerslie Farm in northern Virginia with some of her mother Mary's rescued and adopted dogs.

Susan Heywood of Phoenix, Arizona, works with the Scratch & Sniff Foundation in Phoenix to support regional humane organizations. "We are responsible for what we have tamed," she says. Her poodle, Sedona, is one of her treasured rescued dogs.

Phil McIntyre of Biscoe, South Carolina; his dog, Prince; and Li'l Buck sharing a snack. The stag won't eat from anyone else's hand. "Without him, I guess I'd be crazy," says Phil.

Phil and Prince raised L'il Buck and now go for walks in the woods together.

melting slush roar out of the mountains and down to the mills, one of which you can see from the tract townhouse development where Shannon lives with her stepmother and her daughter, Kennedy.

Mason is pale gold, and although he seems to be mostly yellow Labrador retriever, his grooved forehead, white toes, a white slash across his bull-like chest, and his size indicate something else—Shannon suspects a bit of mastiff.

He was barely a year old when she adopted him from the Oregon Humane Society in Portland, where she learned his sad beginning. "The people who had Mason first had no time for him. They kept him on a short chain with almost no food, and no one played with him," says Shannon.

During the first weeks with Shannon and her husband in their apartment, the canine teenager was a handful. Thrilled by his liberty and all the new sensations, Mason gobbled down everything, including an entire bag of chocolate chips (semisweet, fortunately; dark chocolate can be fatal to dogs), Shannon's lipstick and makeup, a few Christmas ornaments, and a pair of glasses.

Mason was still rambunctious a year or so later, when Shannon, divorced after a year of marriage, was living with her father far up a winding dirt road in Buxton near the coast. It was a good place for big dogs like Mason, and her father, an excavator, raised Tibetan mastiffs there as well.

Shannon worked at Netflix in customer service, and she spent her nights at her father's home, squashed into a twin bed with Mason, a rescued bulldog puppy named Emma, and a cat named Honeybee, who insisted on sleeping on the pillow at Shannon's head. Occasionally the foursome was too much for the bed, and Shannon plopped onto the floor.

One morning about 2:00 a.m., Mason started barking. Shannon, a heavy sleeper, didn't wake up at first. When she did, she was annoyed with the agitated dog. "I told him to be quiet, and he did for a little while, but he was shaking," she recalls. "He got up and jumped on me and barked again. I finally looked out my bedroom window, and flames were coming out the trellis above the window."

Faulty wiring had sent sparks shooting from an electrical box, and the heat was so abrupt and intense it had already melted the smoke detectors in the prefabricated house. Shannon and the dogs ran into the night. "Emma tried to stop and eat cat food as we ran out, and Mason went back and nudged her to make her follow," says Shannon.

"At first, Dad thought I'd already gone to work and assumed I was not there," she says. "He would have had to go back inside to get me if it had not been for Mason."

As it was, her father tried to re-enter the house for the other animals. "Dad got our five dogs out, then he went back. He pulled at the front door, but there was no oxygen inside and it slammed because of heat. He tried again and it just opened and slammed—he didn't know what to do."

It took the fire department forty-five minutes to get to the house. "Then the water truck wouldn't fit up our driveway, which is a half-mile long and curves uphill, so they had to park at the bottom and run hoses all the way up. And first they had to disconnect the main power source. Then it took another hour before the water started to put the fire out."

By then little of the structure was still standing, the ceiling had caved in, and most of the walls were gone, and the smoke had killed three cats—two belonging to her father, as well as her darling Honeybee.

"I sat in Dad's truck with Mason and Emma while we were waiting for the fire truck," she says. "Mason was worried about me, licking my face and lying in my lap. He's always been able to tell when I'm sad. I knew the cats were hiding inside the house. I felt terrible; I thought I should go open a window for Honeybee or something."

It was a terrible blow to Shannon, who has always been around a variety of animals. Her mother owns golden retrievers, while her father has had horses, cows, peacocks, and pigeons. Her grandmother owns rescued border collies and also helps a feral cat coalition.

Shannon has always had nurturing, caretaking impulses: she once rescued a bulldog bitch that had been relentlessly bred, had fungus growing in her wrinkles, and was living outdoors with no shelter. "I found she had so

"It's their unconditional love, and having that is really important," says Shannon, on the site of the house fire.

many respiratory problems that she had been on steroids," says Shannon. "I paid $800 for her, and $2000 in vet bills later she died, but in that time she was so much happier. I am glad I gave that to her. I have her ashes; they were one thing I got out of the house that day it burned."

Shannon seems quiet, almost curt on the phone, but is shyly welcoming when we meet her, and the outgoing Mason seems to lend her a bit more social courage. She doesn't know what her next job will be, but she hopes it might be in a veterinarian's office.

Mason needs more room to run than a townhouse provides, so he mostly lives with an uncle at a nearby farm up the road, while Shannon and her baby share the townhouse with two teenaged stepsisters and Jinx, a long-haired white cat, as well as eager little Harley.

Having a daughter has changed her life, but her bond with Mason remains intact. "I was concerned I wouldn't love a baby as much as I love animals," she admits. "There were times during the pregnancy I wasn't in love with her."

"I find it easier to be friends with animals than with most people," she confesses.

"It's their unconditional love; no matter what your situation is in life or what things you have going on, they are there, and having that is really important."

She strokes Mason's leonine forehead. He pants and grins. "He's always been a best friend to me, more than people. With animals, with Mason, I know somebody loves me no matter what; it lifts my spirits in dark days. He makes it better; he makes me smile."

16

CHOOSING HIS BOYS

TRINA MARVIN, HER SONS, PRESCOTT AND DAWSEN,
AND THEIR DOG, NICKEY

"WE LOOKED AT twenty or thirty dogs," says Trina Marvin. "I didn't want Nickey, and Nickey hated us. He barked, he bit, but my son insisted. He was relentless."

Nickey was found on a California golf course when he was just a year-old pup. He stayed in an animal shelter for seven months, setting a record of unadoptability through his intractable crabbiness and nipping. Nickey wanted to choose his people, and nobody was right.

Then Trina, a golf pro in Thousand Palms, California, and a single mother of two boys—Dawsen and Prescott—arrived at the shelter. For Dawsen, it was love at first bite. He was smitten with Nickey, who is low-bodied, high-headed, and trots with his chest thrust out, his long hair the probable legacy of a papillon, and his sassy attitude certainly a bit of terrier. His tail forms a complete circle of fine hair lofting over his back. And he looks shrewd and smart and dauntless, a small dog with a Napoleon complex.

Nickey was found on a California golf course when he was a year-old pup. He stayed in an animal shelter for seven months, setting a record for unadoptability.

For Trina, appreciating and loving Nickey took much longer. Dawsen was three and a half when Kiko, Trina's beloved Akita, was killed by a drunk driver. "We were so close that when I was pregnant with Prescott, Kiko had a sympathetic pregnancy—her milk came in and she started nesting," says Trina, who has the trim, muscular arms and legs born of her profession, and narrowed eyes as if she were always squinting in the intense desert sun.

"I wanted a Sheba Inu, another Japanese breed that reminded me of a miniature Akita," says Trina. "On a camping trip in Santa Barbara, I saw one and started talking to the owner. The next day we went to his campground. I loved the dog, and the family let Dawsen play with him. And Dawsen said, 'Yeah, but what about Nickey?'" They looked at twenty or thirty dogs, and Dawsen kept saying, "Yeah, but what about Nickey?" So they returned to the shelter, where Trina was certain the nasty little guy would be gone.

"But there he sat, and he hated us just as much as in the beginning," she says.

Dawsen, ice blonde with startlingly light-blue eyes, is reserved but quietly adventuresome. He sat down next to Nickey and talked to the irascible dog for hours. He got bitten. He kept talking.

Trina and her husband had divorced, and Dawsen and Prescott's father moved to Washington State. Dawsen deeply missed his father, and he was especially bereft. "Mom, what do I put in the hole in my heart?" he asked Trina one day.

And he kept visiting Nickey whenever he could persuade his mother to drive him to the little strip mall where the shelter was located. Finally, Christine, the shelter owner, suggested that Nickey go home with the family for a trial weekend. Out of the shelter, Nickey was an altogether different dog: his crabby disposition vaporized, and he was cheerful and engaging and loving.

Now Nickey wrestles with Sylvester, the family cat. He romps with Dawsen, and out in the yard watching Prescott, he provides a first alert better than any electronic security system. His attitude of tender, willing alertness is girded with a fierce protectiveness over both boys. When Trina mock swats either one of them, tiny Nickey charges at her, growling, and he once leaped up and pulled her shorts down to get her away from the boys.

His first loyalty is to his boys, yet he treasures Trina too. When she suffered heat exhaustion and was in bed for a week, he would not leave her bedside. "I don't think he even ate," Trina says. "He drank water, then he went immediately back under the bed."

At bedtime, Nickey barks in the boys' bedroom until Trina lifts him up to the top bunk where Dawsen sleeps. "He allows me to pick him up and put him on Dawsen's bed for awhile, even though he's afraid of the height," she says. "Then I ask, 'Are you done? Do you want down?' He inches over to me on his belly and allows me to take him down."

"Nickey is one of the best things that ever happened to us," says Trina. "Go find the boys!" And Nickey does.

17

TOUGH LITTLE WING NUT

CHRISTINE MADRUGA AND THE DOGS OF THE PET RESCUE CENTER

CHRISTINE MADRUGA IS giving us a tour of her suburban animal shelter, inciting a happy pandemonium among a pack of small dogs. Sisters Ni Ni and Chi Chi, two saucy golden Chihuahua mixes, scamper out of their enclosure, then tear back in, guilty clowns giddy with life, with human attention, and with their own tiny daring.

"They're the baby girrrrrrls!" Christine coos at the ecstatic pair. Ni Ni tunnels under a pink bath towel in her pen, hides for five seconds, then springs out, yipping, five pounds of faux ferocity.

"Chihuahuas are real popular since that Taco Bell commercial—that's why we have so many," Christine explains. "These were two of fifteen dogs we found in a closet in an abandoned house where squatters were living. Ni Ni and Chi Chi were pregnant, and they had their puppies here, and the babies are all placed."

"I taught 'em to wave and smile. Baby girrrrlls! Smile!" she commands. And the speedy little sisters draw back their lips to reveal miniscule teeth and lift little paws stiffly in the air.

Christine Madruga rescues small dogs, dogs used for pit-bull bait, and feral dogs, and she is very careful about who adopts them.

In addition to Chihuahuas, rescued cats, kittens, cocker spaniels, and miniature pinschers sleep, eat, and play in clean, portable wire pens in the middle of the linoleum floor or in steel cages ranked against the walls. Christine's shelter, the Pet Rescue Center, is one fiercely air-conditioned room at the back of a strip mall overlooking a dry wash that might be a riverbed if it ever rained here in California's Coachella Valley.

"Stop barking—the neighbors will get mad!" she orders, and the pack goes quiet for all of ten seconds.

Christine is round and petite, with sunburned legs and arms revealed by her clam diggers and sleeveless blouse. On this hot, bright desert morning, silver heart earrings flash on her earlobes, more silver hearts adorn her watchband, and silver hearts wink up from her black loafers. She brushes futilely at the animal hair stuck to her knees.

The Pet Rescue Center was just four small cages in the back room of an animal clinic when Christine opened it in 1998 in the desert suburb of La Quinta, where luxury homes and golf courses are gobbling up the date and orange groves. Since then, she has taken in 1,389 dogs and 2,036 cats. She has placed them all except for Ni Ni and Chi Chi, who will remain her personal "grrrrrrrls," "grrrrr-grrrrs," "grrrr-gens," or whatever affectionate nonsense words she feels like calling them.

She is also keeping Honey, a Chihuahua mix with fine cream-colored short hair, large ears, and the huge sad eyes of a roadside velvet painting. Honey cowers in a pen, lying on a plush, oval dog bed next to a toy hedgehog. Along her spine, large pairs of sores are healing. "She's about a year old, a real feral dog," Christine explains. "She was running the streets of Indio for six months, and the feral males raped her, used and abused her. Some kids grabbed her and burned her with cigarettes. Finally a lady captured her and brought her here."

In 1975, when Christine was sixteen, she left her family in Long Beach, California, to stay in La Quinta with a girlfriend. She never went home. "Much to my parents' chagrin," says Christine. "They had visions of Cal State Long Beach, but I was a hippie chick."

She found a cottage in Thousand Palms for a hundred and twenty dollars a month and lived off her garden, spending money mostly for fifty-pound bags of dog food and twenty-five-pound bags of cat food for her pets and a huge bag of carrots to carry in her truck and feed to horses whenever she saw one.

When her cat was injured in the fan blades of her old pickup truck, Christine negotiated with the local veterinarian to paint and organize his office in exchange for emergency care. She had been working and studying to be a gardener, but she started skipping her horticulture classes in order to watch the vet perform surgery; she learned how to crop a dog's ears, thread needles, read lab tests, and give vaccinations.

Today, along with her "right arm," a friend named Jean Landes, she runs the shelter by cobbling together donations of supplies from friends, grants from the city of Indian Wells, and gifts from two major donor families.

Dogs find their way to Christine through people who spot them in the street and the desert. She finds dogs tied to the shelter door, and boxes of kittens set on the sidewalk with no notes. And not long ago, a Labrador-dachshund mix and her seven puppies were left in the adjacent alley in one-hundred-and-ten-degree heat.

"Las Brisas? How long have you had her? Is she house-trained?" In addition to escorting us around, Christine is questioning a woman who has walked in with a small stray. She is also managing to direct a handful of volunteers from a vocational service who have been helping this morning, serving scrambled eggs to the dogs, cleaning cages, and petting the pet-able.

"Those guys are not kid-friendly—don't go back there." Christine warns a visiting family away from cages at the rear of the room. "Elvis is back there. He bites everybody!"

"I *am* organized; it just doesn't seem like it," says Christine, whose cheery directness makes her a good ringmaster in this small-critter circus. "Yeah, I go five ways from yesterday, but I love what I do. And I can multitask like crazy."

When Christine places a dog, the two often stay in touch. Cruiser, an escape artist, fence climber, and tunnel digger, comes in each morning with his adoptive mom to walk other rescued dogs. Cowboy "writes" postcards to Christine from Alaska, where he travels in a motor home with his new family. Ernie's owner walks in wearing a tiara. It is her fiftieth birthday; she and her husband are celebrating by heading to Las Vegas. Ernie, an honored alumnus, will stay the weekend at Christine's shelter.

And then there is Bonfire, a small, dark dog whose tongue lolls out through the broken spars of his teeth. He was found behind a restaurant, bloody and chewed up. He had rolled in sand to stop the bleeding. From the bite marks on his body and head, Christine surmised he was a "dummy dog" or bait dog, one of the small dogs used to tease pit bulls or tossed in a dogfighting arena where pit bulls kill them for practice. The little dogs are force-fed tequila, and then their teeth are torn out or broken off. They are sometimes suspended in a tree and dangled above the pit bulls like a living lunch. No one knows how he escaped.

Bonfire has been adopted, but he returned to serve as master of ceremonies for the shelter's annual golf tournament, which raised seventeen thousand dollars that year. His new owner, Minde Parks, had lost custody of her four dogs during her recent divorce. On Fridays, she came into Christine's shelter to pet dogs, walk dogs, and play with them. One day, the small, toothless mutt was there. "I thought he was so sweet—he put his paw in my hand when I put it in his cage," she says. "His story ripped my heart out. I had a dream about him and called Christine and she said, 'He's just waiting for you to come back and get him.' He came home with me, went to sleep on the bed with me, and never looked back."

Minde, an equestrian, named her dog after the 2000 Olympic gold-medal-winning dressage horse. Now Bonfire flies with her up and down the West Coast as she does business, selling wholesale investment products to stockbrokers for an insurance company. He sleeps on her pillow, rises with her at four o'clock every day to drive two and a half hours to the stable where she keeps her dressage horse.

"Bonfire is funny, he makes me laugh, he has so much energy—he grabs stuff and piles it in the middle of the floor," says Minde. "He has given me back an awful lot. I tell his story to every person who reaches out to pet him so people will know what goes on. It's mainly in the Latino community: you see them in the spring and fall; men hook pit bulls to a cart and put rocks in the cart and run the dogs along the road. Guess what they are training them for?"

Bonfire is terrified of big dogs, and windpipe damage causes him to cough if he tries to run. His tongue hangs out of the left side of his mouth, he can't lick easily, and because he has only his rear teeth on each side, he holds bones with his paws and chews at the back of his mouth. He doesn't want anyone to touch his face.

"The first time I gave him a cookie, he was so excited, he put it between his paws and worked on it," Minde says. "Some horrible person took his teeth away. If that had happened to a human, it would be, 'Woe is me; I can't eat,' but he went on. He is so forgiving. He's very excited to meet whoever walks by; he wants to say hello, he doesn't hold grudges, he's happy."

In return, Bonfire boosted Minde out of her post-divorce slump. "I was devastated after losing my dogs in the divorce," she says. "My horse and my dog pulled me through, because they give me so much love."

The need for animal love doesn't stop when the humans involved are homeless: Christine was volunteering at the Coachella Valley Rescue Mission in Indio one Christmas when Jim Lewis, the director, told her that homeless people who have animals were not coming into the local shelters because shelters don't allow pets.

She charmed a contractor into pouring a concrete slab in the Rescue Mission courtyard, donated four kennels, and wrangled donations of food and veterinary care that animals might need while they are there. Now homeless people and their best friends have indoor shelter for five days or longer, and they are less likely to camp out with their cats and dogs in the tamarisk trees and under the freeway overpasses.

Christine's Pet Rescue is undoubtedly the smallest of all the valley animal rescuers, but she claims to have a faster turnaround because this is her passion. Not that animals are released casually: she makes all adopters sign

Re-socializing a puppy at the Pet Rescue Center in Coachella, California.

a contract, raise their hands, and swear an oath: "I promise to love this dog the rest of my life no matter what. I promise never to leave the door open. I promise to keep it until the end of its life."

"They sleep in your bed, they are members of the family, or they don't go home with you," says Christine.

She screens prospective new owners on intuition alone. "I'm a tough little wing nut," she says. "I don't do in-home checks. I go on my gut. Some people will pull up to the shelter, and I'll say, 'Here's a big no.'"

"If I don't like you, you are out of here. One day a woman I'll call Cruella de Ville walked in, and she said, 'I want *that* dog,' and I said, 'Let's see if she wants you.' She said, 'Don't you want to get rid of these dogs?' 'No, we place pets.' 'Well, I want that dog because it matches my decorating motif. I demand you give me that dog right now. Do you know who I am?'" Seconds later, Cruella de Ville walked out, huffy and dogless, threatening legal action.

On another day, a mother and daughter arrived at Christine's shelter. They told her, "We have an outside dog, and now we want an inside dog." "WHAT?!" Christine bellowed. "It gets a million degrees here in summer. I wouldn't give you a Beanie Baby. You better leave now or my talons come out."

For now, and only for a moment, the fierce protector of the small and hapless settles into the corner of her shelter in what she calls "the cuddling chair," an old green armchair, with a castaway Chihuahua in her lap. More dog hair rains down on her pedal pushers, but she doesn't try to brush it away. She strokes the small dog. She is happy; he is happier.

"I think I was a Chihuahua in my last life, I really do. My maiden name was Waugh, you know—Chi-Waugh-Waugh," she says. And Christine laughs.

18

INSANE ABOUT ANIMALS

THE LADIES OF THE OTHER ELIZABETH AND GRISELDA THE CAT

WHEN JEWELRY DESIGNER Elizabeth Locke lost Marvin, her favorite cat, she put out the word for another gray male. Not too long afterward, a kindhearted friend of Elizabeth's who was delivering Christmas baskets to the needy drove up to a trailer in the hills of northwestern Virginia. Out came a gray cat followed by its owner.

"That's a beautiful cat," said the basket lady.

"Do you want it?" said the owner.

"I guess so!"

The friend left the gift basket, scooped up the cat, sped off, and called Elizabeth.

And with that, Griselda the backwoods stray leaped into the silk upholstered lap of Southern luxury.

Today Griselda wears a leather collar studded with petite emeralds set in gold, a gold insignia dangling from the collar, and she snoozes on a Louis Vuitton steamer trunk in the sunny window of a shop with glowing jewelry displayed beneath crystal chandeliers amid Fortuny velvet table runners.

Griselda revealed her true character immediately. "The day before Christmas, I woke up and couldn't find her anywhere," says Elizabeth. "We tore the house apart, and there in the middle of the dining-room table was Griselda, all curled up asleep in a big silver punch bowl as if to say, 'This is more like it!'"

"She also promptly had a honeymoon with a tiger-striped tomcat in our garage and had seven kittens," she says. "Griselda's husband, Walter, now lives in the barn, and their daughter, Walter Jr., lives in the office at the store."

The store is the Other Elizabeth, a jewelry shop in Boyce, Virginia, that Elizabeth has transformed into a replica Venetian palazzo replete with trompe l'oeil stenciled floors, St. Mark's lion banners, and a four-poster bed covered in Thai silk. Jeweled collars and leashes for two imaginary cheetahs named Precios and Tesoro hang on the faux-marble walls. And the "other" Elizabeth—Locke's imaginary twin sister, the Contessa—has strewn silk stockings and a lacy garter belt on the edge of the claw-foot bath tub.

This stage-setting-cum-personal-animal-shelter was conceived of in the mid-1980s, when Elizabeth, then a writer for *Town and Country* magazine, was sent to Bangkok to write an article on the goldsmiths of Thailand. She did more than write about the craft: today her own jewelry, a fusion of Italian classic design and nineteen-karat gold and gems executed with Thai finesse, is sold in twenty-seven Neiman Marcus stores worldwide and at her store on weekends. Elizabeth buys gems in Germany, the United States, Italy, and India, and she lives two or three months each year at the Peninsula Hotel in Bangkok, where she supervises the creation of her jewelry.

The Other Elizabeth may be the only haute couture jewelry atelier in the world where the owner and her staff share their working quarters with cats and dogs. Griselda is the reigning store cat; she knows when it's Saturday and parks herself next to the cat carrier at Elizabeth's home to make the five-minute drive to the store. There she sprawls on computer keyboards, walks across fax machines, swats the computer screens, and preens herself on jewelry display cases, "looking up and down the street in

Griselda lives in what may be the only jewelry atelier in the world where the owner and her staff share their working quarters with rescued cats and dogs.

hopes somebody will admire her. She's so pleased with herself; life is good," says Elizabeth.

Griselda is also not above improving the coiffures of lady customers. "Put your head down there, and Griselda will do your hair," says Susan Mathews, a blonde, buxom southerner who manages the Other Elizabeth. And sure enough, Griselda gently reaches up into my hair and pats, tugs, and rearranges it to her liking.

A former school teacher and self-confessed frustrated actress, Susan is suited for this off-Broadway theater set. And she enjoys sharing the showroom with the diva of Virginia catdom. "She's an old soul, this kitty," Susan says, affectionately stroking the gray cat. "She was svelte until she had her kittens, then she spread like bad margarine."

"She's nothing but an appetite with eyes," Susan adds. "I fix cappuccino, and she hears the machine and waits for milk."

Elizabeth—the real Elizabeth—is tall, model-thin, quick-spoken, and can unleash an enormous smile. She confesses that she was creature-crazy from childhood. "My mother was afraid to come in my room for the spiders," she says. "I'd put praying-mantis cases in my underwear drawer and forget them, and they'd hatch in the spring. I had every creature there's ever been. All my life I've had cats, and at the moment we have three in the office, two in the house, four back-porch cats [including a son of Griselda's], and three barn cats, and one dog named Archibald."

Elizabeth's indoor cats sport jeweled collars with gems that Elizabeth chooses based on what she believes looks best with the tone and color of each kitty's fur: rubies, sapphires, or emeralds. Walter Jr., for example, sports a collar with a canary-yellow diamond.

Elizabeth and her husband, John, a county commissioner, occupy a country estate on the hills above the Shenandoah River that houses guinea fowl, exotic chickens, and horses, relics of a riding phase that she says has passed.

Elizabeth and John have no children. "Children are dog substitutes," Elizabeth decrees, sounding as if she's only half kidding.

"I have never purchased a cat; either they were rescued, they walked up the drive and moved in, or I got them from shelters," she says.

The four ladies of the Other Elizabeth bring four dogs and three cats to work with them. In this species-integrated workplace, the rescued animals include Skitzy, a runt belonging to Elizabeth and John; Marshall, a German-shepherd mix thrown from a truck and now owned by Caroline McKay; and Stoutman Simpson, a sixty-five-pound beagle mix owned by Tricia Simpson.

"Stoutman is the love of my life," says Tricia, who refers to him as S.M. "We do nothing without each other. His main physical attribute is a muffin butt. So I drew him wearing goggles and a cape to hide his big butt. And Elizabeth had a bright orange cape made with a purple 'S.M.' and a jeweled, black stand-up Elvis collar. He loves his cape and will wear it for anyone, but he's not so crazy about the 'doggles'—dog goggles."

Scarlett O'Hara, an American cocker spaniel that Susan purchased, was not rescued, but her cat, Bruisie, came off the side of the road where she had been dumped with two littermates. "She weighed thirty grams on a jewelry scale, and we fed her milk replacement," says Susan. "She lived in my daughter's bathrobe pocket." At work, Susan tucked the kitten into the warm canyon of her décolletage for several hours a day as well.

Gillian Russell brings Duncan, her sprightly West Highland terrier, to work. She also rescued a horse, a Lusitano-Thoroughbred gelding from Portugal, where he was beaten into submission or kept in a stall "until he was unrideably crazy," she says.

Together, the women of the Other Elizabeth have formed a nattily dressed, beautifully coiffed, bejeweled, and big-hearted rescue posse. "When we hear about an animal in trouble, we're all in the car with Havahart traps and trying to get them to the vet," says Tricia. "We are all insane about animals."

Abandoned dogs Max and Skipper found a home for life with Pat and Bob Reever. Skipper had been hit by a car, left untreated, and was found in a shed when her former owners moved. She weighed only thirty-six pounds and spent four months in a clinic.

Max misbehaved around potential adopters, but once the Reevers decided to keep him, he became a model dog.

19

KINDNESS IN THE BLOOD

PATRICIA AND BOB REEVER AND THEIR DOGS, TURTLES,
BIRDS, AND HORSE

"POOR, WEE SOULS," she calls them in her Scottish brogue, but are they ever lucky dogs. Patricia Reever is referring to Petunia, the black beagle mix; Annie, the one-eyed beagle; and Skipper, the incontinent bluetick hound. She means the bottom of the barrel, the unwanted, the costly, the demanding, worst cases.

Patricia and Bob's home in a wooded suburb of Washington, D.C., erupts in Scottish romantic femininity—there are floral cushions and sofas; castles, sheep, and border collies on the china; even checked curtains in the tack room of the small stable in the garden (although the mice eat them, Patricia confesses). The two-hundred-year-old kitchen table hails from a Scottish farmhouse, and a painting of a collie and a lamb hangs above the mantel, where a wood-burning stove throws off a Highland warmth that makes the numerous afghans unnecessary but no less charming. Around the split-level rambler, pea-gravel paths wend through a deeply recessed garden blooming with enormous magnolia trees, gardenia bushes, hosta, and azalea.

Pat's place is the repository of last resort for animals no one wants—or wants to pay for. And Skipper is among the worst. "Nobody will ever take her," says Pat, none too sadly. "She had been hit by a car, and she needs her bladder expressed two to three times a day. Her pads were abscessed and she had nerve damage. She can't be indoors. I took her one afternoon and it turned into ten years."

Skipper now lives in an air-conditioned garden room with skylights, a chandelier, a movable doghouse (built by Bob), a fan, and a cobblestone floor that Pat scrubs and bleaches daily. "Watch out, she'll pee on you," she warns as we attempt to pet the eager hound that shimmies up, tail wagging.

Not all the creatures are so social or as mobile, however.

Polly, a tan-and-cream lemon beagle that shakes and staggers as the result of a car accident, mostly ignores people.

"I've never heard her bark, and she had very little expression on her face 'til about a year ago," says Pat, who took Polly in five years ago. "She looks as if she used to drink a bottle of whiskey a day. She never made eye contact for years, did you, Polly darling?"

In the garden are two box turtles—Petunia and Marigold—once starved so badly they had rickets. They bulldoze about under a layer of leaves in a long, low cage.

"Ah, the wee box turtles," Pat coos as Bob stirs the leaves, prospecting for the turtles. "Technically we are not supposed to have turtles. Technically they are wildlife, but their legs are so twisted they can't dig below the frost line to hibernate, and crows attacked Petunia and pecked her foot off."

The turtle foot amputation alone cost Pat three hundred dollars in veterinary fees.

And when it comes to cost, consider Annie, a beagle that had been battered in the face, resulting in a cracked nose, a broken jaw, and a pulped eye. When Pat took her in, she was pregnant with oversized puppies that had to

Patricia Reever takes in cats and dogs that are unwanted, elderly, or have serious medical needs. Cavalier, an Appaloosa gelding saved from the meat market, became her daughter's show horse. Now retired, he lives in the Reevers' yard.

be aborted. Her jaw had healed so that it would only open one inch, and prior to corrective surgery, Annie was fed via a tube through her throat. Annie's veterinary fees in less than a year came to nine thousand dollars. Now she can eat normally, and although she blinks constantly, she clatters up to guests, cheerful and eager to be petted.

Annie, like many of Pat's rescues, has forgiven humans. "I'll never understand it myself. I think that's why I love them so much," says Pat, who uses love of animals as a kind of psychological litmus test for the people she meets. "Whenever I meet someone who doesn't like animals, I wonder, are they a cold person?" she says.

The Reever household also includes Hagar the Horrible, a rescued love bird that mostly loves to bite everyone. He shares a room in the walkout basement with two meek, giggly ring-necked doves named Matthew and Samuel that were abandoned at a clinic by their owner.

Under the towering maples in the backyard is their largest rescued animal: Cavalier, an Appaloosa-Thoroughbred gelding. The Reevers acquired him from a veterinarian who had bought him for a dollar a pound—the "kill price" for horses being sent to slaughter—at an auction where the vet bid against the Cavalier dog food company. Cavalier put in his years as a show horse for the Reevers' daughter, Janette, and now, at twenty-four, is arthritic but still sassy. Cavalier fixes his shrewd old eyes on Bob and flaps his freckled lips for treats, and Bob capitulates, handing him some bits of carrot.

Not all their animals are hard-luck cases: there is, for example, Max, a small German shepherd mix. "There's no reason nobody adopted Max, who is perfectly healthy and so dear—he was rescued from drug dealers," Patricia explains, and it seems impossible in a world of Pat's making that there should be such things as drug dealers or unclaimed dogs. "I had fifteen dogs at one time, poor souls. They looked like the walking wounded when they went outside," she says, laughing.

In Pat's experience, animals are surrendered or abandoned for many reasons, some solid, all too many specious. "A lot of people call to say they're moving, they have allergies; most have pathetic reasons," she says. "They just can't be bothered, or when we get the dog, it turns out the dog may have cancer. Also, there are some genuine reasons: some people have to go to hospice. And there are battered wives who call, heartbroken, and a woman whose mother has Alzheimer's and she was worried for the safety of her poodle too."

How does Pat pay for the acupuncture ("I just take 'em in for a tune-up," she says), the vet visits, the surgeries, the special meals, the occasional desperate call to a pet psychic? Initially, a friend made a substantial grant to her when Pat became a rescuer. And then there's Bob.

"My husband's very good to me," says Pat, with a twinkling smile at Bob, who is compact and blonde like her, and who looks quietly proud as she talks about their menagerie. Bob manages historic renovation and construction projects in and around Washington, D.C., including the Eisenhower Center, the National Archives Center, and the Supreme Court building. They met in a pub in the western Scottish coastal village of Campbeltown, where he was stationed in the Navy. In Scotland, Pat notes, there may be less awareness of the need for spay-and-neuter programs than in the United States, but dogs are a part of life, allowed on buses and in pubs.

Pat recalls, "As a wee, wee girl, I would cry to see the lorry go to the slaughterhouse, and I couldn't swallow meat." She has avoided meat for the past twenty-five years, and even Bob (a former hunter) converted to vegetarianism long ago. "At Christmas dinner now, it's something tofu," says Pat. "My husband says anything that breathes, that has life, he's not eating it." "And I feel better," says Bob, referring, it seems, to both his body and his conscience.

Kindness to creatures runs in the Reever blood: their son, Scott, is a policeman, and their daughter, Janette, is field supervisor and animal humane control officer for the Loudon County animal shelter. Janette met her husband, Brad, a Washington, D.C., policeman, while they were both chasing down a stray pit bull in the city.

It was Janette who rescued Petunia, the stray beagle, after tracking her for three months through alleys and gardens. The dog had a serious mammary tumor, which Pat and Bob took care of, explains Pat, rubbing Petunia's "hairy, wee belly."

"She looks like a wee, hairy woman who'd be the kind with tattoos, a beer, and a cigarette, and chatting up the men in a bar," Pat teases.

Pat and Bob do not wear leather and do not buy cars with leather seats. When Janette scheduled her wedding, says Pat, "It took me four months to find non-leather shoes that looked nice. It took longer for the shoes than anything else." The Reevers don't have grandchildren yet. "Janette says, 'When babies come out with a tail and fur,' they will have children," says Pat.

Each year, their dogs Annie and Max, adorned in a frilly collar and a bow tie, respectively, accompany Pat and Bob to The Bark Ball, a fund-raiser given by the Washington Humane Society. "It's a formal dance with six hundred people and three hundred dogs," says Pat. "There's not a dogfight the whole night. The dogs get along great lying beside each other."

In their turn, animals have given Pat a purpose for her life and a network of friends in a new country. "When I was first in the States, I was so lonely," Pat confesses, as we sip hot tea in her kitchen. "I'm a people person, so I tried working in an office. I couldn't do it. I tried some of the women's clubs, but it wasn't for me. A friend told us about a dog adoption organization, and I became a volunteer. There I felt as if I was doing something worthwhile."

Pat and Bob have fostered hundreds of dogs in the decades since then. Some died in their care and some went happily to kind homes. Not all of them came from poor households or drug users. Daisy, a tiny Sheltie, belonged to an attorney with a large, luxurious home, Pat says. When the police arrested him for embezzling, they found a dog "unconscious in a basement that was all feces and urine," says Pat. "She looked like a wee Frank Purdue chicken—she was seven pounds, all hairless, and so starved and dehydrated they didn't think she would make it." Daisy recovered with

Bob and Pat, and she weighed sixteen pounds when she was adopted by a Virginia couple.

The phone rings. Pat answers and then explains to us that she will be adding another member to the Reever family. "A family just dropped their seventeen-year-old Jack Russell off at a shelter because he started with seizures," she says. "That just makes me sick; it's a terrible thing to do. The shelter says he's so sweet." Pat looks at Bob and he looks back at her. There is no question between them. There is only an answer.

"It's exhausting, very emotionally draining, but you see the likes of Daisy and the other dogs get a good home, and that's the best thing that can ever happen," says Pat. "To see the dog be happy—that's it, it really is."

"Although humane work is really hard, it is gratifying, and I love what I do," says Hilleary Bogley. "It is an opportunity to help this world with compassion and empathy that we truly need."

20

CLOSE TO MY HEART

HILLEARY BOGLEY AND THE MIDDLEBURG HUMANE FOUNDATION

THE WOMAN ON the phone said she had thirteen or fourteen cats and could the shelter lady come and take them. So Hilleary Bogley asked her for her address.

"I don't know," said the woman. "I never left here."

"Okay, what can you see from your house?" Hilleary persisted.

"The railroad tracks," said the woman, which was not much help because several train lines run through that part of rural northern Virginia.

"Go outside and read the number on the house," said Hilleary. It took more sleuthing than she ordinarily needs to do, but Hilleary managed to locate the woman and rescue her cats.

As founder and director of the Middleburg Humane Foundation (MHF), Hilleary has a job that requires a certain resourcefulness; she is detective, social worker, athlete, and fund-raiser rolled into one.

The foundation occupies a corner of Marshall, Virginia, that is rich with the scent of lilacs in the spring, masking it from the nearby auction barn, a stockyard where Hilleary and friends have claimed many a woeful horse from the meat buyers.

In autumn 1994, with the help of an investment group, she opened the MHF, a four-and-a-half-acre remnant of a farm surrounded by weeping crabs and willows. Her office is a late-eighteenth-century log cabin with additions that house a laundry, kennels, and cat runs. Last year, more than seventy animals from chickens to horses found shelter here or in MHF foster-care homes. On average, most rescued creatures are sheltered here for two months before being adopted by the person Hilleary hopes is the best match for them, but there are permanent residents, including a three-hundred-pound taciturn black pig named Otis. Otis naps in a shady shed, raises his head when she calls to him, flaps his considerable ears, and then turns around and goes back to sleep.

"He arrived ten years ago from a townhouse in Old Town Alexandria, where he had his own couch and watched TV," says Hilleary. "He loved Oprah Winfrey, and he'd run up to the TV and lick the screen when she appeared. But neighbors were not happy about Otis, and when his owners lost in court the right to keep him, he found a home at the shelter."

"Otis was devastated at the difference, and grumpy at first out here," says Hilleary. "He was hard to show as an adoptable animal, so he ended up being an opportunity for us to tell people that these pigs are farm animals: unless you can provide an enclosure like this, don't get yourself a pig."

Born to a banker father and a beautiful, jet-setting socialite mother, Hilleary was, she confesses, "a kind of hyperactive only child, a bad kid." Her father died in a foxhunting accident when she was four. At five, and for many years thereafter, her best friend was Samantha, a German shepherd. Hilleary's wild behavior got her bounced out of college, but she finally graduated from a veterinary technician program. In addition to her work at the MHF, she serves as humane investigator for Fauquier County and Culpepper County. It's a job with a degree of danger and the certainty of seeing things that are disgusting and depressing, and one she manages with diplomacy.

"What I've found in many cruelty and neglect cases is that it is a way of life," she says. "They got a chain dog—a dog on a chain 24/7—because their daddy had a chain dog, and their children are going to have a chain dog. That's just what they see as normal. At least we got an ordinance passed that the chain has to be three times the length of the dog's body, including the tail. That was very important, and they have to have shelter, and the area has to be clean so they don't eat their own feces."

"These people never had a dog in their house, and they are outraged at the thought of it being part of their family. When I suggest it, they look blankly at me and say, 'That dog ain't coming to my house!'" she adds. "The dogs supposedly serve the purpose of protection, but I find that baffling, because most of the time they are chained in the back, and how much protection can they give on a seven-foot chain?"

Sometimes the salvation of both the animals and the people attached to them comes in tiny, edible increments. "I try to educate the kids in these places that when I come back, if the dog has fresh water, I'm going to bring cookies," says Hilleary. "I'm not a kid person, but I know it's important to teach them empathy."

If Hilleary's shelter deals with a range of animals, it deals with an equally large range of people. There are the just plain misinformed, such as the toothless man in camouflage gear who walked to her shelter with three dogs. He was such a great believer in feeding his animals garlic that one of his dogs nearly died from its blood-thinning effects. He had a unique treatment for parasites too. "My daddy taught me to feed 'em deer meat and then run 'em real hard and fast, and the worms don't get no time to latch on," he told her.

Sometimes it isn't ignorance but fear that causes the abuse and neglect that she sees. "People have lost control of their own lives, and the only thing they have control over is an animal. 'That animal drinks when I let it drink and eats when I let it eat,'" she says, managing not to sound angry. "It took me three years to figure that out. Why would this family in a warm, cozy trailer, each one of them fifty pounds overweight, keep their dog starving and freezing in the yard? It all comes back to control."

Many but not all of the problems stem from people who are uneducated and whose lives are impaired by drugs, alcohol, and unemployment. "As a whole, most of the people who are respectful of themselves and their homes are also good with animals, but more often than I like to, I see some very wealthy people who have large horse farms and don't give a damn about the cats," she explains. "It really blows me away. There's a beautiful horse-breeding facility here with literally hundreds of sick cats on the property. We offer to go in and spay and neuter, and the owner doesn't want us to spay any females; she doesn't want to spend a penny on the cats."

Before she returned to Virginia and started the MHF, Hilleary volunteered at a shelter in Denver, Colorado, euthanizing animals on Tuesdays and Thursdays for two years. "That's a part of my life I wish I could not remember, an evil necessity of society," she says. "They were using lethal injections into the abdomen, which was painful and took several minutes. The people doing it were never trained properly, so as a licensed vet tech, I offered to train the staff. I remember crying the entire time, every time I did it. One of the animal holders told me, 'You need to get over it.' And I said, 'The day this doesn't bother me is the day I want out of the profession. And if it doesn't bother you, you should move on.'"

Things are getting better, she adds, noting that the Colorado shelter now operates under a different euthanasia method and policy. "But until there is state legislation that requires mandatory spaying and neutering or some type of licensing for people that choose to have animals to breed, they won't have to be responsible. And so many other things in this world are higher priorities."

As Hilleary walks around the shelter property, a tawny oaf galumphs by her side, the first dog she's adopted for herself in a dozen years. A genial mix of pit bull and Great Dane, Melvin was one of a litter that Hilleary rescued at a trailer park where she delivers food to needy people as well as to dogs. "Hookworm and freezing and anemia—it was so bad, one of his siblings died on the way home with me," says Hilleary. She gave the drug dealers twenty dollars for the pups. They wouldn't sell her the mother. "Sometimes I have to take them back once I fix them up; otherwise, if I piss them off, I can't get back in. And in two or three months they have a new pup chained out there."

"This is our problem-child pen," she says, introducing a wiggling, barking, and leaping trio of large young dogs: Patrick, Emmett, and Oliver. Oliver's former owner was slowly slicing off his nose and feeding him sugar water until Hilleary managed to pry him away from her. She doesn't let such atrocities eat her up any longer. "I can come here and be productive, and then I can go home and eat and watch TV," she says. "In twenty-one years of humane work, I've learned to focus on the good."

The shelter's current horses include a mare named Maria; her yearling son, Bugs; and Julie, a small chestnut filly. Their sleek coats and bright eyes give no sign of their troubled past. "Julie was shot with a pistol," Hilleary says. "The family bought a horse for the mother who was dying of cancer. She died and they lived with filth, alcohol, and drugs. The dogs were chained, and the three horses were emaciated, kept in wire and garbage and car parts. They never saw a vet or a farrier; they were never de-wormed. Bugs has wounds from being beaten with a chain. For a long time, he was so injured he just leaned against things to stand up. I scheduled his euthanasia three times and cancelled it three times. He finally started to gain weight, and I gave him another ten days. Now he's one-hundred-percent sound, a beautiful quarter horse, and a woman just adopted him. The people who did that to him were never prosecuted."

The office of the shelter has small, sunny open-air runs with climbing ledges for cats, a laundry, and rows of immaculate interior cages with a view of a bird video playing for the indoor cats. The core of the building is the chinked log house—the oldest four-room cabin in Fauquier County, Hilleary says. She lived here for eight years, sharing the bathroom with Jose, the shelter assistant, until she could afford to live elsewhere.

In the cabin loft, a pure white mother cat nurses a litter of four white kittens and an orphan gray kitten who stretch pink toes and tiny pink bellies luxuriously in the sunlight. We settle down on the floor to watch the kittens cavort. The mother purrs and blinks at us in welcome.

"See is waisin' da widdle orphan," says Hilleary, lapsing into a high baby talk as she strokes the cat. "Oh, I don't know why I do that," she laughs. "I speak that way to cows by the side of the road."

"Animals are close to my heart; they give me everything," says Hilleary, her voice thickening with something more than she can articulate. "A house is not a home without a cat, without four-legged creatures. Although humane work is really hard, it is gratifying, and I love what I do. It is an opportunity to help this world with compassion and empathy that we truly need."

21

RICKIE'S HUGS

KATHY SCHROEDER, HER DOG, RICKIE, AND PETS ON WHEELS

MOST DOGS SIT up for treats, their paws dangling, their eyes fixed on the snack, their mouths moist in anticipation of a reward for the trick. Rickie sits up as a greeting, a welcome, and a blessing. He rises perfectly vertically, sitting flat on his neatly-trimmed bottom, spreads his front legs wide and invites and enfolds. He presses his face against your chin or chest and hangs on to your shoulders. "He likes to give hugs instead of kisses," says Kathy Schroeder, Rickie's owner. "I just have to share this embrace." So after working hours, Kathy and Rickie visit nursing homes through a program called Pets on Wheels, a one-woman, one-dog mobile hugging team.

Kathy is a little person, a perfectly proportioned adult measuring four feet seven inches, and she looks exactly in scale arriving at this suburban Scottsdale, Arizona, nursing home in her Morris Mini Cooper. A bright blonde wearing jeans and a spotless white polo shirt, Kathy has powerful forearms from wrangling animals through the suds, combs, and clippers at the pet-grooming service where she works. She opens the car door and out

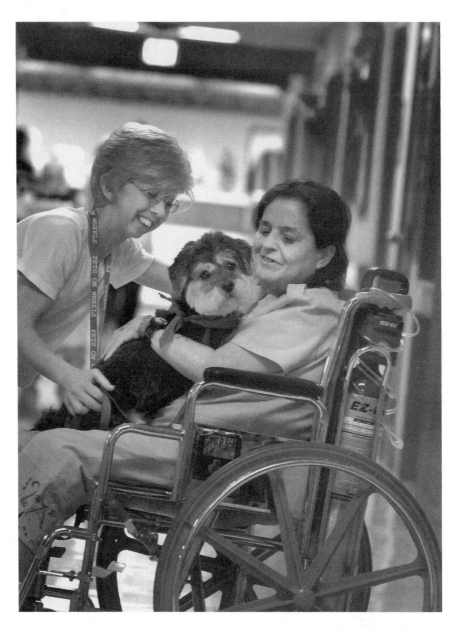

Kathy Schroeder brings her rescued dog, Rickie, to visit residents of a nursing home. "I have a lot of depression. I just lift up when he comes," says Phyllis Youngblood.

bounds Rickie, a small gray-and-white mix of schnauzer and Lhasa apso with a big white mustache and enormous wet, dark eyes.

The petunias at the door of the home are parched by the desert valley wind, and inside the smell of popcorn drifts through largely still, empty halls. Dim, plain hospital rooms, most lit solely with the greenish glow of television, branch off the hallways. In a large interior lounge, a lone rabbit crouches in a cage, a cockatiel sits silently in another small cage, and half a dozen women in wheelchairs silently watch a movie. "I come here because I worked with animals for eighteen years, and I know what effect they can have and how people miss them," Kathy explains.

Phyllis Youngblood, a small, dark woman with scarred forearms and face, rolls out to meet Rickie. Phyllis was struck by a car a year ago and has been a resident in this home for a year, nine months of that time with a tracheotomy. She reaches for Rickie, and he puts his paws on her chest and presses his forehead to her chin. There is no licking, no fawning, just an immensely loving presence, no treats needed. "I have a lot of depression. I take things for it, but I just lift up when he comes," says Phyllis with a wet cough. "He's a special guy." Above and below Phyllis's green medical wristband, crude tattoos are visible on her arm and hands. A long pale scar travels from the left side of her forehead across her brow and cheek. "He's just a big lover; he visits me many times," she says happily.

"It's hard for people to understand that you don't just take any dog and go visiting," says Kathy. "It has to be the personality of the dog. You really can't train them to do this, just like you can't train certain people to want to go and visit. And it develops more over time. It didn't take him long to pick up differences in leashes to do the visiting or for regular walks. Now he gets really excited for Pets on Wheels, and he grabs the leash."

Rickie was in the Maricopa County animal pound in February 1996 when Kathy and her mother arrived. Her mother had persuaded Kathy to look for a dog: two weeks before, her golden retriever, Honey, had died of bone cancer. In the chaos of barking, whining, and leaping dogs, a little dog sat and wagged his tail, not begging but greeting her. "That one," said her mother, and Kathy paid the sixty-dollar adoption fee and took him home.

Kathy acquired Rickie before she married. Her husband, Terry, brought to the marriage a seventy-five-pound rottweiler mix named Nesha, and the sixteen-pound mutt and the strapping hound are best playmates. Terry, who works as a hot-dog vendor in Mesa, is petite like his wife, a man born with dwarfism.

Rickie will not tolerate tension, says Kathy, including marital discord. "If Terry and I are getting into it—not fighting, but if we just raise our voices—he goes into a closet," she says. "It makes me feel bad."

Kathy believes Rickie has what she calls "little angel wings," and it's hard to disagree. "My whole family did a lot of praying about the kind of dog I was going to get," she recalls. "I was really blessed to find him; he is special. I believe it was arranged that I could have him."

This evening, Rickie also works his magic on Mark Sanchez, who is just a year old and not much bigger than the dog. Mark enters the lobby with his grandparents, Maria and Ramon, to visit his great-grandfather. The family lives in Guadalupe, one of the poorest neighborhoods among Phoenix's sprawling desert communities. Mark is so excited to see Rickie, who sits up, gravely inviting him to hug, that he dances on the tiptoes of his new sneakers.

"He had a little Chihuahua, and two weeks ago, big dogs attacked it and killed it," says his grandmother. "They are usually chained up but they escape. He named him Rufus, and he asks for him. And Mama tells him Rufus is bye-bye."

Mark crushes Rickie to his purple football jersey, jiggles him, and pats him with so little control that it verges on the violent. Rickie, in his green bandana, tolerates this with his usual wide-eyed calm. To a boy who has lost a puppy, this small pet is a balm, if only for the moment.

"With animals, it's true, unconditional love," says Kathy, squatting down on the linoleum to watch Rickie and Mark. "If you have a bad day, they don't care. They don't care what you look like. They are happy. It's just neat."

Rickie is not just a hug on four legs; he's a pretext for conversation or a warm moment in otherwise uneventful lives. "I like to watch the interaction between people and animals," Kathy says. "With a lot of the people we visit, you get some conversations about the dog and about pets they've had. That's good because it gets their mind off of things going on."

The things going on too often include dying, says Kathy. "We visit people for years, and the next time we come they are not there," she says. "It's some relief for them, for what they were going through, a lot of pain." She pauses, "And you miss them too."

But while they are here, Rickie and Kathy provide a measure of happy distraction for those they visit.

"Rickie gets their mind off things, even if it's for ten or fifteen minutes," says Kathy. "When you hear somebody say, 'I've been waiting for you all week; you are the best thing that happened to me all week,' it makes you want to do it more. You see you really are doing something that makes a difference."

Angel, an injured umbrella cockatoo, wears a prosthetic beak.

22

EILEEN FLYING

EILEEN MCCARTHY AND MIDWEST AVIAN ADOPTION
& RESCUE SERVICES

WHAT PEOPLE SHOULD know before they get an exotic bird, according to Eileen McCarthy, is this: it's like having a three-year-old with a sharp object you can never take away. And this child—who is tireless and has a voice like a siren when provoked—requires room to run fifteen to twenty miles a day. He has special needs. And he lives for thirty-five to eighty years.

In other words, for most humans, keeping an exotic bird captive is a very bad idea. But that has not stopped thousands of people a year from buying birds, only to find out just how difficult it is, and then abandoning them at a humane society, an animal shelter, or worse.

Eileen is the founder of The Landing, an exotic-bird shelter in St. Louis Park, Minnesota, the country's largest shelter in terms of number of birds, and on this afternoon, it sounds like it. The decibel level inside the three-room storefront is piercing: finches beep and cheep; dozens of cockatiels, macaws, lorries, conures, lovebirds, and parakeets chirp, whistle, and shriek; and at the top of the racket are raw, furious yells from a bossy, blind cockatoo named Sam who wants only to be petted—interminably. "RAAAAAACK!" hollers Sam in a raw, angry tenor that rises above the chorus.

Eileen is statuesque with burnished mahogany red ringlets and ivory skin. A Celtic bird tattoo of her own design circles her right bicep. Silver lizard earrings dangle above the shoulders of her black T-shirt, four silver rings gleam on her toes, and a tattoo of pastel baby elephants parading trunk-to-tail decorates her left ankle. She arrives toting a couple of her own pets: Abby, a green Quaker parrot, and Mango, a sun conure the color of a blood orange, ride on a perch in a ventilated black mesh backpack.

"Hello, Papa," says Abby.

"Abby started this whole thing," says Eileen, freeing the pair to waddle and flutter around her office. "He came from a person who didn't want him, and he was a little monster, yelling and biting. But I didn't know that. I thought it's just a little bird; how hard can it be?"

"What's up?" says Abby.

"Now I know," says Eileen.

Since the shelter opened in 1999, Eileen, her sister, Jamie McCarthy, and volunteers have cared for fourteen hundred unwanted, abused birds. Behind their streetside office are two rooms warmed by low-hanging, full-spectrum lights. In the first room, half the residents are cockatiels, finches, and parakeets with medical problems or that are not tame or whose mates have medical problems. The other side of the room is home to "the sweet guys," says Eileen, birds that are immediately adoptable.

"People don't come here to adopt little guys, but they are great talkers. A parakeet holds the world's record for bird vocabulary—two thousand words," she says, moving through her rainbow-hued aviary. "Cockatiels, parakeets, and lovebirds are throwaway pets to some people, because they are inexpensive and they are impulse purchases."

Eileen releases a pair of bright-scarlet lories to rove the room: Amelia, a female chattering lory, swoops onto my shoulder, whispers nonsense in a crackling, demonic voice, then nips painfully at my ear and snatches at the corner of my lips. Rasta, a male black-capped lory, lands in my hair, gnaws on my ponytail holder, and refuses to be dislodged.

"I think I begin to understand Alfred Hitchcock's movie *The Birds*," I say, appealing to Eileen for help. "Yes, the more time I spend around birds, the more frightening that movie is," she says, laughing.

In each room of this suburban aviary, large cages are bright with toys and perches, Popsicle sticks and toilet-paper tubes (for chewing), spiral ropes, bells, hollow balls, leather wreaths, and debarked branches—veritable playgrounds for birds. Eileen threads her fingers through the toys into cages where birds with beaks like wire cutters eye her.

"Step up," she says, opening cages and offering her hand. "Talk to me," she says, and "Wanna snuggle?" and "Oh, come on now, be gentle."

"My childhood dream was to be like Doctor Doolittle, to talk to the animals and to figure out what they are saying," says Eileen. "The first animals I was aware of as a kid were elephants. When I saw how they suffered, I stopped going to the zoo and the circus. I'm a bit of a crusader, maybe it's the Irish in me. The Irish have to be against something!"

Her first cockatiel died prematurely, and a second one flew away, so Eileen set herself a moratorium: "No more birds until I do it right." The need for rescue that she saw as a member of a bird club inspired her to organize something on a larger scale, and Midwest Avian Adoption & Rescue Services (MAARS) was formed. "When I started MAARS, I thought it would be more effective to work on felony provisions in the state animal anticruelty statute. But it doesn't have the same rewards as when you make a direct impact on an animal's life. It's emotionally harder, but I like making a tangible difference right now—not waiting years and years for people to get a clue and get legislation passed."

The problem with tropical birds is, well, people, says Eileen. "People don't understand: these are wild birds even if they have been raised in captivity. The stores that sell them don't have knowledgeable staff, or they don't care. Here are sweet, docile, cute, and dependent baby birds, but they mature and have minds of their own and become challenging, and wild behaviors surface. Birds have the intelligence of a two- to five-year-old child, a special toddler that is never going to grow up. People are completely unprepared for that. One of the most common statements from those who surrender birds is, 'If I had known then what I know now, I *never* would have gotten a bird.'"

Tropical birds are now covered by the Animal Welfare Act, and the United States Department of Agriculture has jurisdiction over birds not used in food or research, and regulates standards for keeping birds in captivity. But for most birds, Eileen explains, anything we provide is woefully inadequate. "A macaw in nature flies twenty miles a day, so what should be a minimum size for an enclosure?" she says. "They are lucky if they get a cage twice their wingspan in every direction."

"Hi, Zac! Now just be gentle," she greets a flaming scarlet macaw with a tail more than a foot long. "He's only two and a half. He's been naughty with me. It's not natural for them to bite. In the wild, they are prey, and their defense is to fly away. But he loves Jamie, my sister."

"Hey, Bogie," she says, opening the next cage, where a demure white bird sits. "She's an eleven-year-old bare-eyed cockatoo from North Carolina. She's here because her owner's husband got colon cancer. Her boyfriend is Chief." And Eileen opens the door on the adjacent cage, where a bulkier cockatoo perches, his crest fanned up and forward over his face. Bogie clambers up to him and begins to preen his wings.

"Chief likes young women, the younger the better," says Eileen. "When twelve- to fourteen-year-old girls are here, they are his favorite. We don't know how he knows age, but we think macaws have terrific vision, and possibly he can see age differences that way."

Bogie sets to work humbly nibbling Chief's forehead and neck. He sits regally, accepting this grooming as his due.

"Chief is wild caught, which is not legal anymore," she says. "He caused us to take the position they should not be pets. He is *so* unhappy. When he first lived with my sis, Chief built nests for Jamie, was solicitous of her, and wanted her to come into the nest. He would be furious if she came home after dark."

She opens the cage door for Malachi, a Moluccan cockatoo that has so severely pecked out his feathers from stress that his naked gray breast skin shivers visibly over tiny ribs. He doesn't like to come out, but she opens the door anyway. "We don't know his history, but the damage to the follicles is so bad the feathers won't grow back," she says as Malachi eyes her. "It's like people with mental illness; the behavior becomes compulsive. They can't stop." Tiny doses of antidepressants have been used successfully to treat the compulsive behavior, she explains, but they are not effective in all cases.

Stress for birds can include neglect, loneliness, changes made that separate them from their flock, and lack of stimulation or social contact. They withdraw, they pout, they pluck and self-mutilate, they pace. They scream incessantly and shred their bedding and toys.

Zoe, a tiny Goffin cockatoo, was kept alone in a cellar for two years. She tore at herself, using her beak and claws to reach every feather except a few on her head. She lives at The Landing now, but her behavior continues, and she is skeletally skinny. Her bright black eyes alert and full of determination, she pads about on Eileen's shoulder, nuzzling her ears and hair, chattering affectionately. Without feathers, she cannot fly and occasionally plummets to the floor, where she looks like an anorectic young chicken that somehow escaped from a roasting pan.

Some of Eileen's other birds—many of the birds that have been kept in tiny cages—don't know how to fly.

Andy, a male umbrella cockatoo, was neglected after his owner became pregnant, got married, and moved. He became lonely, then angry, and unlike mild Malachi, he turned his rage outward. "Open up!" he would demand.

"He was so aggressive, he was almost crazy," says Eileen. "He would rattle the cage and scream and throw himself against the bars. When he realized he was going to get let out and paid attention to, he became the sweetest bird. Now I trust him more than any cockatoo we have."

"Uh-oh," says Zac, and Malachi barks like a dog.

Adoption costs for birds from The Landing range from twenty-five to five hundred dollars, depending on size, but the purchase price is the least of the obligation. "The best thing for a dog or cat is to be in a loving home, but for birds it's not the best thing," Eileen explains. "We need to work on preserving them in the wild. These are not pets; we can never meet their needs. You wouldn't have a dolphin in your swimming pool or a panther in your living room—it is obvious to most people that it's wrong. If you keep a dog in a little kennel twenty hours a day, that would be wrong, yet a bird in a cage is acceptable?"

Eldo, an umbrella cockatoo, went through four adoptive homes and was returned each time to The Landing because the people developed allergies to him—a common situation, Eileen explains, because of a natural powder that coats birds' feathers.

"Hi, Sam." She greets the blind bird that is padding comically flat-footed on a towel on the bottom of his cage.

"Pretty bird," Sam says in a Popeye-the-Sailor voice.

"Yes, you are a pretty bird. Do you want to cuddle?"

"Hello, Sam," says Sam.

Jamie arrives, a paler, younger version of her sister, and takes Zac into the office to play. She works in human resources at a major foods corporation and helps at The Landing many additional hours a week.

"Whatcha doin'?" says Abby.

Zac toddles around amiably on the floor, alternately allowing Jamie to pet him and flinging balls and a yellow stuffed bird around. He carefully tastes each of her fingers, running his black leathery tongue daintily from cuticle to tip, and she picks dander from his broad red brow.

"Mmmm, good," says Abby.

"I have a special place for captive wild animals, and how they suffer angers me," Eileen says. "We humans have the chance to go to a therapist; we have power to change things if we have that desire. No matter how much desire animals have to change their situation, they cannot. They are powerless. The Christian Right says we have dominion over animals. No, we have stewardship, and we'd better use it responsibly and with reverence for that animal."

"When you see something that isn't right, it's your obligation to do something—that's how we were raised by liberal, hippie parents," she explains.

Thousands of people buy exotic birds only to discover how difficult they are and then abandon them, says Eileen McCarthy, founder of Midwest Avian Adoption & Rescue (MAARS) in Minneapolis.

Eileen is married, Jamie is single, and neither has children. They are exercising their own wings these days. "Our mom was emotionally dependent; we couldn't separate from her and be free," says Eileen. "When she died, it was freeing—I didn't have to live for her too."

"I find it so enraging the way people overlook birds. Birds have always been a symbol of freedom, yet we want to possess them, put them in cages, objectify them." She knows this life firsthand, she says.

"I've struggled with many demons and disorders," says Eileen, who prefers not to name them for fear she would be stereotyped. "I was the smart, pretty bird in a cage pulling out my feathers and knowing that something was terribly, fundamentally wrong with me and my world, yet helpless to make it all right. I was imprisoned by hideous flesh and the desperation and futility of easing my mother's pain, and bearing it myself and suffocating from rage, fear, and loneliness. I was certain of only one thing—that I was meant to fly."

When she chose to go into animal advocacy, she considered circus animals—elephants were her first love—and then dogs and cats. But she loves all creatures. "I went to see *Jaws*, and I cried when they shot the shark," she recalls. "He was only doing what he was meant to do."

And she made a conscious choice to enter the much less visible world of rare birds. "I could have chosen dogs and cats, and then if I wanted my life back, there are others who would take over. But with birds, there wouldn't be anyone. They are extraterrestrial, not mammals, and they are so alien to us; that's why I think they are so overlooked. There is such a huge disconnection between people and birds. It's why people abuse prisoners with hoods on or keep slaves—you can tell yourself they are different, so what you do to them doesn't count. I identify, having been a little different myself."

And then there is the return on the effort. According to the McCarthy sisters, love from a bird is not unconditional as it is with dogs, cats, and horses. They say, however, that the relationship can be much deeper than with mammals.

"It's a very intense and more equal relationship than with a dog," says Eileen. "Birds actually learn our language, and if you are a good owner, you learn theirs."

"And don't think they don't know what they are saying," says Jamie. "They really hold conversations with you. If you want to befriend a macaw, talk to them about themselves; it never fails. Chief nods his head appropriately when I tell stories about him."

The birds also converse in human language with one another—at least in fragments, according to the sisters. Dmitri, a rescued blue-and-gold macaw, said "shut up" to the cockatoos. Other macaws at The Landing learned it and taught still more macaws to screech "shut up" and "knock it off" and "shut up, Bongo" to Bongo Bob, a cockatoo, and to a remodeling crew next door. And the cockatoos would scream back in voices meant to carry miles through the jungle. It sounded like a fight on a playground amplified through microphones. "You shut up!" "No, you shut up!" "No, you!"

As we walk around the aviary, Eileen continues to let birds out of cages, to stroke them and toss them gently toward their cages so they flap their wings. This is not just fun; it's training: the sisters receive many birds that first learn to fly here.

"Fifteen years ago, I was exhausted and disgusted and started to believe that it would be easier just to surrender—to let go and let the dark emptiness devour me in eternal silence," says Eileen. "But I hung on. Through my mother's illness and death, I held on as tight as I could, so much that it hurt to breathe, until one day it all made sense. It was me all along; I was the key to unlock my cage. And I did. I opened the door, put one foot in front of the other, and I have never looked back."

"All I need of the past, the little girl I was, my mother—I carry them all within me now. They are the ones who seek out the caged birds and nurture them. I am the one who teaches them to fly."

Lucy Warner Bruntjen with Beagley, the last dog saved by her late mother, Mary Warner, who exposed a nationwide pattern of pet theft and trafficking in stolen dogs.

23

MARY'S LAST RESCUE

LUCY WARNER BRUNTJEN AND ELLERSLIE FARM

BEAGLEY IS A small, shy dog that keeps to herself. She learned a lesson about trust long ago, and she lives her lesson daily. Beagley lives on Ellerslie Farm outside Berryville, Virginia, a farm founded in 1869 by immigrant Scots, and stout Black Angus cattle still graze on fields that roll from the low, white country house to the nearby floodplain of the Shenandoah River. Miles of four-rail, white wooden fences converge below the house at a small bridge over Chapel Run, a trout stream running dark as milk chocolate with spring rainwater.

As our car tires crunch up the long gravel lane of ancient yews and white pines and into the circular driveway, the compact little beagle takes an obligatory sniff of air and beats a retreat through the holly bushes around the guest cottage. In seconds, we see her trotting away into the cow pasture, her paintbrush tail tipped in black, her back legs scissoring through the grass.

While Beagley flees from us, her buddy, a large Doberman-Shepherd cross named Pup Pup, stalks forward gravely. His black, almond-shaped eyes with no whites give him the somber look of an Egyptian jackal god, and his impassive face is hard to read. Are we going to be bitten, we wonder? But no, he stands while we stroke his head and neck and pat his firm back.

Beagley is the last surviving dog rescued by Mary Warner, godmother of frontline fighters for pet welfare, who died in May 2000. Her husband, Leon, who owns Pup Pup, lives here now, ailing and in his nineties.

Lucy Warner Bruntjen, their daughter, opens the Dutch door of the kitchen to meet us and walks us through the kitchen and out to the terrace: frothy yellow forsythia and low, fleshy striped hellebores are blooming. Vast blossoming crab-apple trees and daffodils wave thickly along the low field-stone wall facing the Shenandoah River. We admire the land with Lucy, an artist who is tall with straight silver hair, flushed cheeks, and an ageless kind of innocence and enthusiasm seldom seen in adults.

The old house smells like cream and black tea, and it is full of animal images: a LeRoy Neiman panther print hangs in the dining room, another Neiman—a hunt scene—hangs in the living room near Mary's grand piano and surrounded by bright floral sofas.

"Mom took in every animal she could. The vet or the game warden would call, and if it had been hit in the road, she paid for the surgery or the amputation," says Lucy. "We had a dozen dogs sometimes and three or four three-legged dogs here at a time, including Boogley, a male beagle. He lost the leg he used to stand on to pee. He never could make the switch to standing on the other back leg, so he did a handstand—he stood on his front paws."

Dogs ran free on this farm, and so did the Warner children: Lucy, her sisters, Julia and Mary, and her brother, Lee. "We learned to ride by playing cowboys and Indians and hide-and-seek and having galloping races," says Lucy.

When Copper, Mary's beloved German shepherd–bloodhound cross, vanished in 1968, she began to gather articles, compile statistics, and assemble fliers about missing dogs until she had neat spiral notebooks filled with information from other grieving pet owners. She set up headquarters in the "Dog House," a converted spare room off the garage. She took calls and logged sightings of strange men with trucks who used chains and bait. Something was happening to pets like her Copper, and she wanted to know what it was.

Finally, she put an ad in the newspaper inviting those who believed their dogs had been stolen to meet at Ellerslie Farm. That night, her house was filled with bereft, distraught, and enraged pet owners.

Over time, Mary's meticulous logs showed a pattern that pointed to extensive, international dog theft. "For the first ten years, no one except the owners believed her," says Lucy. "She had to work very hard to build up credibility." It was a situation no one wanted to believe.

Lucy leads us to the dining room and spreads out the dismal map her mother created on the table. It shows a concentration of dots—reports of missing dogs—up and down Interstate 81 on the East Coast. It is the trail of men with trucks stealing pets and buying animals from pounds and selling them to research laboratories, dogfighting rings, and furriers. The markers cluster densely in the map of surrounding Virginia counties: Tazewell, Giles, Wuthe, Buckingham, Hernci, and Louisa. Then they trickle outward, north to Ontario, Canada, and west all the way to the Simi Valley of California. The trail of markers crosses the Midwest, and I note markers near my hometown, Albert Lea, Minnesota, where our dachshund, Bruni, and other neighbors' dogs vanished one day in the early 1970s.

Mary started a group, Action 81, named for the corridor used by many dog thieves or "bunchers." She produced files containing "fifteen years of human agony, tears, heartache, nervous collapse, anger, nightmares, and the unrelenting question: why doesn't someone do something?" she wrote.

We leaf through her thick spiral-bound reports: "1974–1993 Theft of Dogs and Cats in the United States," "The Dealer Lab Connection," "Theft of Dogs and Cats Report," and her newsletter, *Voice of the Missing*. The newsletter assembled information about "thieves, bunchers, dealers, illicit pound operators, legislative attempts and failures, some successes, USDA ineffectiveness, occasional effort, law enforcement apathy, deliberate turning away."

Part detective as well as researcher, Mary pursued information, well, doggedly.

"Mom sneaked into pens and crawled through dog doors; it was crazy," says Lucy. As she closed in on the theft rings, Mary received death threats and notes threatening to burn down the Warners' stable.

One evening at a gathering where she was speaking, word was delivered to Mary: "There is a bomb in your car." Mary finished her talk, left the building, and started up her 1974 red Volkswagen Beetle with the bumper sticker: "Lab Animals Never Have a Nice Day" and drove home undaunted.

She appeared on ABC's *20/20, 60 Minutes,* and Connie Chung's show, and she presented a paper on her data to the National Academy of Sciences. And she marched up the steps to the state capitol in Richmond and changed Virginia law so that out-of-state trucks couldn't enter Virginia and pick up dogs from the pounds, so researchers couldn't go to pounds and buy dogs, and so stolen pets wouldn't end up dying in laboratories. Within a year of its passage, the 1981 Virginia dognapping law reduced the rate of pet theft by half.

Cleveland Amory of the Fund for Animals presented Mary with the Polar Bear Award (named for his cat) in honor of her work. It stands on an antique wooden chest in the hall, along with a wooden sculpture of a howling coyote that Mary and Leon bought in Colorado. "Mom said that coyote, with its mouth open crying, represented the suffering of the animals," says Lucy.

Even music—Chopin in particular—spoke to Mary about the anguish of abused animals. "Mamie loved his passion and compassion and his minor key," says Lucy. "When she played Chopin on the piano, she said it was connecting with the suffering of the dogs."

The last dog Mary personally saved from suffering was little Beagley, who came to the Warner family a dozen years ago. "The pound called Mom because there was a frightened little dog abandoned on the street, and people had been trying to catch her for two years," says Lucy. "We don't know what happened, whether she had been stolen for lab use and escaped, or got lost from the pack of a local hunt. After Mom caught her, she lived in a pen here, and Mom took her for walks, but it took years for her to build Beagley's trust. She would just sit and quake; she was so afraid of people, of being locked in. Mom would put her on a retractable leash, and she would just fly out to the end of the leash. Now she's totally free; she's one of the gang."

"Mom was high-strung and tense until she had an animal with her, a dog in her hands; then she softened up," says Lucy.

If animals gave Mary peace, they also gave her purpose right from the start. As a little girl in Minneapolis, Minnesota, Mary Elizabeth Case unhitched the iceman's horse one day and set him free in the middle of the city. As a middle-schooler, she formed a horse-protection society. The first scrapbook she made consisted entirely of animal images for which she wrote captions.

"Her life with animals was bigger than with us; they filled a bigger role," says Lucy, without resentment. "She could never live without animals. She was a worried, anxious person; she lived on adrenalin, and they calmed her, gave her continuity. She needed something to need her."

The Warners moved to the Ellerslie Farm full-time in 1966, in part because the whole family liked to ride. Mary in particular loved horse shows, was a great competitor, and filled the stable with Hungarian Thoroughbreds, quarter horses, and ponies. "Mom would jump things other riders would not jump, and she told her grandchildren, 'If you don't want to jump, you don't have to, but if you are going to jump, ride like hell!'" Lucy says. Mary and Leon rode into their eighties, because their philosophy was, "To keep up with the young people, all you need is a young horse."

Mary's life was framed by dogs and horses, and they were her metaphors. When a grandson asked her, "Mamie, what's the secret to a good marriage?" her answer was, "You've gotta have strong legs and soft hands, and you'll be just fine."

For her children, animals were also a medium of confiding. They had a bloodhound named Dennis, and every night, Mary would go from bedroom to bedroom and ask her children about their day. "And we'd talk Dennish tak inna Dennish da Bwoodhound voish sho you didn't have to weveal too mush," says Lucy, giggling. "Being the dog was like wearing a mask. And when we'd talk Dennish tak, we'd say, 'Go shit down' and then laugh ourselves into hysterics."

"My parents were full of energy," says Lucy. "I know I stayed home too long. I should have rebelled and moved on, but we wanted to do things with them; they were so full of life. And we loved the same things."

So Ellerslie Farm was perpetual summer camp with Leon and Mary as the counselors. Mary organized riding, piano lessons, swimming, and conversation and table-manners lessons, and she kept achievement charts and gave awards. And everywhere there were animals—ducks and geese, dogs, cats, and horses.

"I know I had a different mother than my friends had—she made everything fun," says Lucy. "At her parties, there'd be all these fancy people here, and they'd go into powder rooms, and Mom had put fake dog poops in there. Or she would ride the ponies into the house and around the dining room. And she could make people crack up and howl."

For all the fun, at her core was empathy for animal suffering. Petite, intense, and brainy, Mary never forgot anything, and never got over it, either. Lucy walked into Mary's bedroom one day not long before cancer took her, and found her mother weeping.

"Mamie, what's wrong?" she asked.

"I'm thinking about Aunt Fanny's dog who got run over by a car," said Mary, recalling an event of sixty years before.

Ellerslie Farm is dreamy and remote. Dogs run free here again. And although Mary, the one she trusted most, is gone, Beagley seems happy. The next morning we watch her, bold in her dawn hunt, running over the sloping pastures, nose to the ground, assessing fresh scents: rabbit? deer? Maybe woodchuck! Then Beagley and Pup Pup are gone, over the hill, trotting down by the river, nosing about in the shady banks thick with bluebells.

24

FOR THE TAMED

SUSAN AND BILL HEYWOOD, THEIR DOGS,
AND THE SCRATCH & SNIFF FOUNDATION

WE ARE DRINKING iced tea and hiding from the noon heat at Adobe, a café on the golf course in the plush Paradise Valley corridor of Scottsdale, Arizona. Above our heads, fans stir cool air over the white adobe walls; outside in the shimmering heat, golfers putt on velvety greens, and entrepreneur Robert Kiyosaki (author of the best-selling book *Rich Dad, Poor Dad*) strolls by in golf attire.

"Well, hi, Robert, how are you doin'? How's Kim?" says our host, Susan Heywood, with familiar warmth. She knows Robert and his wife, and what's more, she knows their beloved calico cat, Sweetie.

Susan is a marketing maven who cofounded the Scratch & Sniff Foundation, one of the most effective and organized animal-benefit groups in the country. And the Kiyosakis are two of the people she's enlisted in the cause to make life better for Arizona cats and dogs.

Every day is tough for many animals in this bleached, baked, and cactus-studded stretch of the American Southwest. Maricopa County—the nine thousand square miles surrounding Phoenix and Scottsdale—has often led the nation in euthanizing unwanted cats and dogs. In 2000, for example, the county euthanized approximately 37,000 of the more than 61,000 unwanted pets received by Animal Care and Control. This prompted Susan and her husband, Bill Heywood, to start raising money to benefit pet therapy, shelters, and rescue and adoption organizations. Scratch & Sniff helps these various groups streamline and prevent duplication of services, and the foundation secures funds to get animals off the streets, out of the pound, and in from the desert.

Susan is flat-out glamorous. With her fine black hair, immaculate tailoring, good-but-not-ostentatious jewelry, and subtly perfect makeup, she looks as if she could be Elizabeth Taylor's younger sister. Her beauty derives from her Lithuanian-Jewish immigrant father and Cherokee-Irish mother. The languid, sure tempo and very Southern, very female tone of her voice come from a childhood spent in Oklahoma and Texas. Susan's motto is "Dress British, think Yiddish, talk Southern, and smile," and the result is an effective, warm intelligence that she employs to good effect and noble purpose.

In the high-rolling community of Scottsdale, where couture counts and a cosmetic nip-and-tuck is common if not mandatory, Susan wields her unique blend of warmth and polish to tap into something far deeper than the local passion for surface beauty.

Susan was a successful marketing executive married to one of Arizona's most beloved radio broadcasters when she made a discovery: there were no city animal shelters in Phoenix-Scottsdale. There was Animal Control—the city pound—where an animal had just seventy-two hours to live unless claimed by its owner or fished out by a rescue group. Nearly sixty thousand dogs and cats go through the pound each year.

This fired the mental Rolodex of a couple that knows who's who and how to enlist them in a good cause. In 1997, its first year, the members of the Scratch & Sniff Foundation set out to raise a hundred thousand dollars. Planning took a year, but their black-tie fund-raiser—which managed to attract and entertain a coterie that is thoroughly sick of black tie fund-raisers—brought in double that amount. Susan and Bill and their friends had tapped into something: the desire to help needy animals.

In animal rescue, there are roughly two groups: the hands-on people who feed the castaway or lost dogs and cats, clean cages at humane societies, and wade into the animal-control facilities or into the weeds beside the highway to fetch out the fortunate few. And then there is the write-the-checks group. Susan knows where her skills and abilities lie.

"I couldn't do what those groups do who go into a pound and see sixty dogs (and those are the lucky ones), and then go into the euthanasia area and pick one dog to live," she says. But Susan has helped raise and distribute more than a million dollars to selected humane groups and put a $90,000 Petmobile on the streets to bring adoptable animals into communities.

One year, Scratch & Sniff's board enlisted 550 heavy-hitting animal lovers for the black-tie dinner at the Arizona Biltmore, a Prairie School architectural confection that epitomizes prewar southwestern elegance. Movers and shakers were honored—one was playfully christened "Most in Need of a Leash"—and four valley mayors and their dogs judged a gourmet dog-food contest. For the main entertainment event, the canine connection netted them big-name vocalist Lou Rawls.

"I had been pestering this nice gentleman in community relations at Fox 10," Susan says. "He had met Lou Rawls and his wife, Nina, and Nina's baby is her Pekingese dog, Millie. He said, 'I'll tell him about you,' and so we went from there."

Susan and company know how to throw a party, from the party favors to the auction items, which for this event included a four-course dinner for twenty (it sold instantly for ten thousand dollars) and a lighted miniature carousel (which brought in the same amount). The cohosts were Susan's friends Carol and Harvey Mackay, the businessman turned best-selling author of *Swim with the Sharks Without Being Eaten Alive*. Carol and Harvey have a gray tiger cat named Oscar and a golden retriever named Sunny, and they feed a pack of feral cats and a one-legged roadrunner in the yard of their Scottsdale home.

"There's a lot of I'll-go-to-yours-if-you-go-to-mine, a trading dollars thing in this community," Susan explains. The Scratch & Sniff extravaganza, however, is different. "There's no payback; they do it from their heart, they come to it out of love. There were a lot of political leaders there, and they were supporting a constituency that can't attend their black tie fund-raisers and can't vote for them. It's a very unselfish act."

"Scratch & Sniff did it the first year for the Arizona Humane Society, which was the only rescue group we knew," Susan explains. "Then we found marvelous little organizations that didn't know each other or talk or collaborate, and they were duplicating work toward similar goals."

Scratch & Sniff is poised to become the United Way of pet services without the bureaucracy. To do so, it has had to limit its focus to dogs and cats. Susan and the board scrupulously interview recipients about their methods, their philosophy, and their efficiency at saving and placing adoptable animals.

Later that day, we drive to Bill and Susan's home in a quiet, elegantly landscaped gated community in the Biltmore Hotel area. The sunny townhouse has rich coral and cinnabar walls, black granite kitchen countertops, and Lalique nudes. While we wait for Bill to come home from his drive-time financial show on a local AM station, Susan pours white wine into etched goblets ("some of Grandma's crystal from the Confederate War," she says, and we don't doubt it). And we gratefully settle ourselves onto the couch to be licked by three poodles, Scratch, Sniff, and Sedona. They are, of course, rescues. Scratch and Sniff were littermates that Susan scooped up at the opening of a new shelter run by the Arizona Animal Care and Control. Sedona was a little red runt, the unsold last of ten puppies that was about to be given to the pound.

"Mr. Sniff, we didn't think he'd make it," says Susan. "He had mange and kennel cough, and he had been abused and would shrink from your hand. He'd given up and wanted to die. Now we call him Bubba the Love Sponge or Scratchmo, because he is Sammy Davis Jr. reincarnated. It's 'let me show you what I can do.'"

"I was always dragging home cats, which Mother would give away because I am so allergic to cats," says Susan. "My first dog was a Boston bulldog that Mom named Sinner Girl (Mom was a flapper, what can I tell ya?). Sinner Girl died in my junior year in high school. Later that spring, Mother took me to Oklahoma City, and we got my first poodle, named, of course, Madame Suzette. It's been a long love affair since then, and I've never been without a poodle."

Just beyond the patio, Ernie and Bertha, a South African gray goose and a white snow goose, totter out of the pond and shriek like rusty gates, accompanied by a bevy of mallard ducks Susan and Bill have named Ethel, Fred, and Chester. Susan designed Scratch & Sniff to focus on cats and dogs, but that doesn't stop her from rescuing other creatures.

"One day Ernie was eating out of my hand, and he just fell down," Susan recalls. "When I picked him up, I found he weighed about an ounce, so I took him to the vet. Well, he had a fungus in his bill, and he was starving. I felt so bad that I hadn't seen it before. It took six months of vet care and injections in the breast, but he got better."

Bill arrives home, handsome in a silvering, middle-aged, on-camera guy way, with a soft, round Kansas voice and easy cordiality. Like Susan, his life has been built around people and good causes, and his public has reciprocated: not long ago, he was voted All-Time Favorite Arizona Radio Personality.

But there is someone missing: Susan opens a velvet-covered album containing photos of their beloved bichon frise, Delilah. The queen of the Heywood household, the imp who belly flopped in the fountain at the Arizona Biltmore, Delilah ruled the roost from the leopard-print chair in the entry. She also liked to play ball, but only with blue balls, and when she ran, she dragged little Sedona along, clinging to her hind leg or her tail. "Delilah was the most human and cat-like of any animal I've ever known or had an opportunity to love; she was so sensitive to voices and feelings," says Susan. Then she and Bill go pale beneath their tans. Delilah died of autoimmune hemolytic anemia, a swift and inexorable disease, just two months ago.

Delilah came into their lives when a previous poodle, Mr. Laguna, passed away, leaving Bill and Susan dogless. "Couples our age go through the emotional trauma of losing a pet, and often they say, 'Never again,' so I wrote myself a contract that within a month after losing my dog, I would go out and look for a puppy, because I don't want to live my life with that vacant part of my heart," says Susan. "We don't have a big home, and without the patter of dog paws it would feel like a mausoleum."

For Susan, dogs have been a continuous chain of love from puppyhood to their old age or death, but for Bill, raised on a farm in Kansas, animals just meant searing, repeated loss. Bill's stepfather worked in construction as a bridge builder, and the family lived in a mobile home, traveling the little towns of Kansas from Zimmerdale to Poplin to Woodbine.

"He'd bring home a puppy, and three months later we'd have to move to the next town, and he'd tell me, 'We can't take Snickers; we will give him to the boss,'" says Bill. "I was not able to get attached to a dog, or a place we lived, or anybody at school, so I steeled myself, put a shield between me and anything that mattered," Bill says. "I learned to be very cold, and not to care about dogs, people, or teachers. I was kind of a bad boy."

Around seventh grade, when Bill moved to his grandparents' farm, the loss continued. "I'd be given a horse, and then I'd wake up one morning and ask what happened to Ginger. My granddad or stepdad would say, 'We sold her last night to somebody.' The same with dogs, chickens—everything was disposable."

"I had a beautiful collie, and my stepdad caught her in the chicken house eating eggs, so he took her behind the barn, and I went with him, and he shot her between the eyes—boom! And there was a series of events like that up through when I was seventeen or eighteen years old."

Because he was not allowed to rely on people or animals as a child, Bill found stability in basketball. "Sports taught me not to be a selfish schmuck, to learn to care about and play with a team," he says. "I was one of the first sophomores to make the starting five on the high-school team, but I had a habit of quitting on the play. One day the coach, a John Wooten type, told me, 'I will put you so low on the totem pole for that that they will have to pipe light down to you.' So I had to play my way back up through the ranks. I became All-American at junior college, but the lesson was don't quit, don't be a brat, and *do* get attached, because if you don't, nothing means anything."

So Bill is puzzled by the widespread lack of attachment to dogs and cats. "Once a week, the newspaper publishes a graph from the Humane Society on their animal intakes," he says. "People come and go in Phoenix, this is a very transient area, and for every three who arrive, two leave, and the dog is the first disposable thing. They leave it behind like a BIC lighter."

Bill and Susan have been married twenty-eight years, through many dogs, and they plan to keep it that way forever. "Will Rogers said if there are no dogs in heaven, I don't want to go to that heaven, or something like that," says Susan. "That's how we feel."

Chutzpah, caring, and marketing savvy plus Bill's media stardom have helped the couple muster some real muscle toward animal rescue. They recently flexed that muscle when a local wild-animal park was threatened.

"The native tribe owned the land it was on and gave the people thirty days to get out, because the tribe wanted to build an RV park there," says Bill. "There were 365 exotic animals, everything from giraffes to lions and tigers. So I got the owner on the air. We put the word out everywhere: if you've got a truck, saw, hammer, or can volunteer some time, come help them move. And we had people with semitrucks cut holes in the tops of them for the giraffes. Some professional animal movers from the Carolinas drove here to help."

As a result of the publicity, someone donated land in Camp Verde, Arizona, for the menagerie. "It's a much better place, cooler than Phoenix," Bill says. "And there was nothing there to house the animals, so people donated electrical work and plumbing work and built facilities. It was a massive exercise."

Their ability to make those links is one of their strengths. "For us to move the animals along, we have to depend on other humans; animals cannot do it for themselves," Susan says. "I am very conservative in style. To throw blood on people wearing fur coats is not part of my philosophy."

In order to bring their work home in a visceral way to potential contributors, Susan occasionally takes them to visit some of the groups supported by Scratch & Sniff. She recently shepherded ten friends to a shelter for pure-bred dogs. They were so moved that they all got on the phones, called friends, and placed half a dozen dogs before the day was out.

She persuaded another group to visit a service that offers pet therapy for blind and sight-impaired children. "Desiree is five years old; she cannot walk, cannot speak, and they are teaching her to crawl," she recalls. "The only thing that will motivate her to crawl is Lizzie, a collie. So they place Desiree at the end of a padded area, and she moves toward the dog. Lizzie herself was trying to crawl to reach Desiree. When they reached each other, Lizzie fell on her face, licked her face, her thick glasses, and for the entire time we were there, Desiree was just wallowing in Lizzie. It helped me and potential funders understand what the dollars are doing, because sometimes we are removed from fieldwork."

And it's the humane fieldworkers whom she admires most, she says. "I spend a couple of Saturdays helping the Petmobile with adoptions, but it's very hard to leave the animals behind, not knowing if they are going to be adopted or euthanized. How do you sleep?"

"I can't imagine life without a dog, without that love as a part of my heart," Susan says. "Everybody says that, but it's their total acceptance. A dog is always glad to see me no matter how I look or what mood I'm in. I reach over at night and touch that fur and have them snuggle up. Without dogs, I think life would be so lonely."

Scratch & Sniff has a T-shirt with the slogan: "We Are Responsible for What We Have Tamed."

"I love that; isn't that good?" says Susan. "If I had a creed, I'd like for people to understand and adopt; that's it. We have domesticated all these dogs and cats, and they are our responsibility now. Some of the people in pet organizations have seen the underbelly of humanity and have given up on people. But if we have any hope to help animals, it's with humans."

25

ALWAYS BRINGING IT HOME

RON DANTA AND DANNY ROBERTSHAW
AND THEIR DOGS AND CATS

THIS IS THE Deep South, the lowland around Camden, South Carolina, weighted by a wet heat so oppressive in summer that farm work begins in early morning and leaves off by noon or two o'clock. Down here even modest homes have a man-made bass pond; grits and green-tomato pickle are on restaurant menus; and gas stations feature a selection of china figurines including the Ten Commandments and black praying hands, as well as bumper stickers that declare: "Possum, the Other White Meat."

Tall pines shoot up from the red sand; mourning doves call amid sizzling choirs of cicadas; alligators sail silently across lakes; and white cattle egrets convene in the trees. And on the flat, rich land where cotton still blossoms just outside the town, at least one family has held on to their plantation for more than two centuries.

Horse trainers Ron Danta and Danny Robertshaw thrive here at their Beaver River Farm, down a lane of young live oaks hung with strands of Spanish moss leading to a low white farmhouse. In the field along the driveway, women in leather chaps and helmets trot and canter horses to the faint songs of mockingbirds and the bantam rooster in the farm's chicken coop. The stable doors are tall and open to the breeze, and each horse is dressed in a plaid fly sheet, its halter buffered in sheepskin.

Ron appears quietly, a blue-eyed, silver blonde, six foot eight inches tall and wearing jeans and a polo shirt. When I step out of the car and stand next to him, the word Viking comes to mind. "Would you like to see the Kitty Hilton?" says Ron—so much for the Viking image, I think—and we follow him over the grass to the side of the stable.

Horses are their business, but rescuing dogs and cats is their calling: on the outer wall of the stable is a spacious cage with carpeted ramps, climbing logs, and napping ledges. A chicken-wire-covered catwalk runs from the large pen up the wall of the stable into the barn itself and spans the stable aisle to the hayloft. Some two dozen cats—orange tabbies, calicoes, and grays—snooze in the grass or on ledges; others hide in the hay.

"Hi, Mama Kitty," Ron says, squatting to stroke a cream calico through the wire. "She is the oldest one, and she has eye herpes that need medication twice a day. We've had her nine years."

"Here's Stachio," he says, pointing out an orange tabby with an orange mustache. "We found him with his dead littermate on the road near Pawley's Island, South Carolina. He had mange and ringworm and was so little he had to be bottle-fed . . . Snow Kitty was up in a tree—we went and got a ladder."

Wherever they go, Ron and Danny keep Havahart traps in their trucks and horse trailers along with Danny's homemade liver snacks, a handy stash for luring frightened dogs off freeway medians, lost cats from restaurant parking lots, and injured and starved animals in trailer parks or the woods.

"We can't pass a scraggly dog on the road," says Ron. "Our hearts just pound, and we drive to the next exit and come back. And at restaurants, if we see them out back by the trash cans, we catch them. We tackle them if we have to."

A slick black dog, possibly with Doberman ancestors, waggles his rump with joy while greeting us and rolls over on his back. "That's Wino," says

Ron. "He was found with a bullet through his heart and lungs, left in a Camden dump in all the beer and wine bottles. We thought he was dead. He is the sweetest dog!"

We are joined by a gold, dingo-looking creature named CJ ("the man used to beat her. She's still scared of men in baseball caps") and Ebenezer, a miniature wirehaired dachshund ("rescued from a Kentucky puppy mill"), who seizes a saliva-soaked, green tennis ball and drops it at my feet. Ebenezer and I play fetch until the ball is so saturated with his drool that it gives off a fine mist when it bounces on the grass.

Ron and Danny spend December through April in Palm Beach, Florida, with their clients at the big horse shows, staying in their second home on Lake Wellington with six of their dogs ("the neediest ones," they say). On the horse-show grounds, the two blonde, tan men—a sort of Siegfried & Roy of the horse world—are a common sight, breezing along in a three-seat golf cart packed with dogs.

They are gods in the equestrian competition circuit. In 1989, Danny won the hunter-over-fences championship at not one but all of the most prestigious horse shows in North America: Devon, the Pennsylvania National, the Washington International, at Madison Square Garden, and the Royal Winter Fair in Toronto. It had not been done before or has not been repeated since. He was the leading hunter rider of the year. And now, despite having lost five discs in his spine to the rigors of his sport, he trains horses daily.

Their clients are women and girls from all over the country. Some arrive via the family jet and drive to the farm, where a crack crew of stablehands make sure their horse is buffed, saddled, and ready. They take a lesson—trotting and cantering in circles and over the barrels, rocks, timbers, and poles in the jump field—with Ron or Danny gently encouraging and correcting. Then they dismount, hand the horse back to the grooms, and are home in time for dinner. Often, the students go home with a dog or cat as well. Over the years, Danny and Ron have matched more than two hundred rescued animals with their clients, family, and friends.

"It's my belief that every animal, like every person, has its own personality, and we are matchmakers," says Danny. "Just like with our horses: we want the temperament to suit the customer or friend. We want them to go somewhere they are loved. We don't push; we just make the animal available, and if the match transpires, you can tell. The friend meets the animal and just has to have the dog or cat. With horses, we just hope it stays sound—our name and reputation as trainers are on the line. Either way, nobody wants it to work more than we do."

"Sometimes we offer the animal because there's a sadness in someone's situation and what we have can fix it," says Ron. "Or there's a void in their lives the animal can help fill."

And to those who adopt the dogs, they often give short pieces called "Rainbow Bridge" and "A Dog Sits Waiting." Ron hands me a copy of the latter.

A dog sits waiting in the cold autumn sun, too faithful to leave, too
    frightened to run.
He's been here for days now with nothing to do but sit by the road,
    waiting for you.
He can't understand why you left him that day. He thought you
    were stopping to play.
He's sure you'll come back and that's why he stays.
How long will he suffer? How many more days?
His legs have grown weak; his throat's parched and dry.
He's sick now from hunger and falls with a sigh.
He lays down his head and closes his eyes.
I wish you could see how a waiting dog dies.

(Kathy Flood, "A Dog Sits Waiting")

Danny and Ron have rescued many waiting dogs. Under the shady cedars and sweet gums near their house, the dogs yet to be adopted and the dogs they are keeping for themselves live in grassy pens with igloo-shaped dog shelters and wooden sheds.

Blue, a foxhound, dances happily around his pen, his bark a loud, wheezy whisper. "He weighed twenty-seven pounds and was so full of ticks that he was very anemic," Ron explains. "He took us four days to catch. And when we got him home, he barked twenty-four hours a day. I mean nonstop! I don't know when he slept."

Blue's kennel mate, Bagel the beagle, scrambles up from a cool trench he has dug under the roots of a tree. Bagel had been hit by a car on the interstate and was lying on the shoulder of the road. "I was driving past and thought he was dead, but he moved his head just a bit," says Ron. "Both his hind legs and hips were broken. And people were just driving by."

Addie is stout and cheery with wide-set brown eyes and short golden hair, and she is still nimble at fifteen. "She was living at Seabrook Island, South Carolina, and she'd walk the seventeen miles from the Texaco station to beg for food at the gate of the island development," says Ron. "The guards at Seabrook had been trying to catch her for years. They finally got her, but when we asked if we could have her, they said no. So we had a couple of women friends distract them, and we sneaked in back of the guard office and took her. She was six weeks at the vet with heartworm; she was in terrible condition. The next year she upgraded her life to our air-conditioned condo at the beach."

Modest granite gravestones flush to the grass pay tribute to the dogs that will never leave: "Chloe Chlo-bird 1995–1996: 525,600 Minutes of Love" and "Moonpie 1978–1994: A Legend."

Danny, who was out on the field schooling clients' horses all morning while Ron taught lessons, changes his shirt and joins us. He is a shorter version of Ron, also strikingly tan, blonde and blue-eyed, except his eyes are bloodshot—he's allergic to cats and dogs. That doesn't deter Danny from keeping abundant animal company. "I just cough a lot sometimes," he says.

He also has a faulty aorta from high blood pressure; not long ago, Danny spent two weeks in the intensive care unit and was prohibited from riding for a year. "So when we were in Florida, I went to the pound once or twice a week and adopted a dog," he says—perhaps one of the first heart patients to use dog rescue as cardiac rehab therapy.

Ron and Danny have saved rabbits and a fawn. They've gone at night and thrown food over a fence to hungry horses they couldn't take home. Around and under one house trailer in the woods, they rounded up seventeen starving cats, sneezing and infected with eye herpes and eating out of trash cans. Armed with gloves, towels, and cages, they went for the whole group. Ron got cat-scratch fever and blood poisoning that time, and then in the hospital he reacted violently to antibiotics and had to be slapped into restraints, raving. They placed fifteen of the cats and kept two themselves.

In the wake of Hurricane Katrina and Hurricane Rita, they hired animal transport to collect rescued dogs from storm areas: eight hundred dogs were fetched from New Orleans and the surrounding areas and taken to their home. From there, Ron and Danny dialed friends around the country to find homes for them.

"We sent dogs home with folks in Pennsylvania, New Jersey, and New York," says Ron. "The real traumatized, real scared ones you couldn't get your hands on; those we took with us to Palm Beach. We ship the dogs to Oregon and upstate New York, and everywhere someone wants one. We have spent more than $15,000 shipping dogs all over the country to new homes. Our accountant says, 'Are you insane?'"

"The one we named Neighbor was tied to a tree during the hurricane—he was just a puppy and wasn't found for four months," Ron continues. "By then he had to have surgery on his neck because all you could see was the buckle on his collar. It took eighty-eight stitches to get the collar out of his neck and fix him; it was awful. Afterwards, I bought a harness for him. He learned to shake with his right and left hands and to lie down. He's just so sweet."

"We have some horrendous cases, but it's so rewarding. The beautiful thing is we never have fewer than twenty-five dogs in the house, and we have not had one dogfight, which I think is amazing. They just know they are saved."

Ron and Danny never regret the cost in injuries or time or pet chow or veterinary care. "Two years ago, we spent more on canine and feline than equine care," says Ron, who once asked a customer to leave their stable because she complained, "If they didn't mess with all those stray animals, the boarding fees here would be lower."

And they never stop squeezing in visits to the local shelter between full days of lessons and training horses. We are lucky to be there when they squeeze in one such visit. After morning lessons and lunch, we join Ron and Danny in their mushroom-silver Excursion and head for the Walter Crowe Animal Shelter, a one-storey concrete building on the outskirts of Camden behind a door flanked by luxuriant rosemary bushes.

"This is what I don't do well," says Danny, looking apprehensive and hanging back a bit as Ron strides into the shelter office.

"Hey, how are you guys today?" asks Heather Williams, a shelter employee. "We've got one for you. It was on the [euthanasia] table, and Sharon said, 'Doesn't this look like a Danny and Ron dog?' And so we took him off the table."

Danny and Ron are the shelter's best customers. At sixty dollars a pop, they have fetched out dozens of pairs of dogs (they allow themselves two at a time—usually). And in 1999, when the shelter closed prior to being transferred from Kershaw County jurisdiction to that of a humane society, Ron and Danny learned that all the remaining animals were scheduled to be euthanized. They hitched up their horse trailers, called friends with vans and trucks, and caravanned to the shelter, coming away with all twenty-seven cats and dogs.

"Here's the dog Sharon saved for y'all," says Heather, holding the leash of a medium-sized black-and-white spotted dog that licks its lips and cowers, tail tucked, and looks up at them for cues. The men crouch down and hug and stroke the trembling animal. "Oh, he's so sweet," says Ron. "What do you think?" Danny asks, looking at Ron. They are silent, stroking the dog together.

Leaving the dog with Heather for a moment, we walk deeper into the shelter: cats and kittens are on one side, dogs in another, and puppies in a third area. Like many animal facilities where convenience and economy are bywords, this one has concrete floors with chain-link partitions, except here a lawn sprinkler washes continuously over the roof of the outdoor kennel to cool it.

Pairs of clean, bright-eyed dogs—tan and gold, black, white and brindle—beg for attention or doze in the shade. A short, sturdy black Lab pokes his paw through the bars toward Danny and Ron, begging to be touched. And two basset hounds, one with pus blurring his eyes, his mate swaybacked with nipples dragging, paddle forward to be petted too. ("She's been bred half to death," Heather explains later. "The owners turned the two of them in here; they just didn't want them anymore.")

"I see you, puppies; yes, you are very cute," says Ron, bending over pens where black puppies and tan puppies knock over their teddy-bear toys, plush ducks, and chewed blue-plastic food dishes in a hurry to get to him.

"Oh, you look just like Pancake," says Danny to one of them. "That was a dog we found in the road. We named him that because if we hadn't picked him up, he was going to die of pancake disease (getting flattened by traffic)."

"How are you doing?" I ask Danny.

"I was better before I came in here," he says, his quicksilver blue eyes moist, his jaws clenching and unclenching.

Back in the office, Heather takes a look at the shelter records at my request. I want to know the size of the tragedy here and how much people like Ron and Danny are helping.

"Let's see: in 2003 we got in 4,929 animals; 1,035 were placed and 3,700 were euthanized," she says, scanning a report. "This year, by May, we had taken in 1,631 and adopted out 600."

"Is the black-and-white dog neutered?" asks Ron.

"Neutered, chipped, and vaccinated," she answers.

"How about the Jack Russell that's in with the puppies? He looks kind of rough. How old is he?" asks Ron.

"He's only two, but he is a sexual beast. He was jumping over the wall and bothering the puppies—he needs to be neutered," says Heather.

I suggest that since the shelter is always packed, more animals could be kept longer for placement if there were a campaign to enlarge the building and add runs. "No, we don't want more space—that would mean we'd get more animals, more cost, more employees, more euthanasia, and that's *not* what we need," says Leslie Bruce, the shelter office manager. "We need a really good spay-and-neuter program. We already do a low-income spay and neuter for people that qualify, but there's the macho thing: a lot of men won't allow the family jewels to be touched. And a lot more say, 'They are just animals; who cares? Another one will come along.'"

"And they think it's good for the kids to enjoy the wonders of nature, to see the cat have kittens," Ron adds. "They are country people; they don't go for neutering. They say, 'Oh, my daughter-in-law will take one' . . ."

" . . . and then they leave 'em all running loose," says Danny.

"It breaks your heart, I tell you," says Ron.

The concept of responsibility for life, so powerful in Danny and Ron, is widely underdeveloped in rural areas such as Kershaw County. "We found a litter of kittens in a plastic bag knotted shut," says Heather, "and then someone brought in puppies, and we asked where they are from, and the man said, 'Oh, the mama dog is mine, but the puppies are strays.'"

What about free spay and neuter provided by a mobile truck? I suggest. "That's why we are waiting for the lottery, Ron's parents and me; that's going to be it," says Danny. "Our goal and dream is that—and to open a shelter where animals can live out their lives no matter what."

Camden is not the only place Ron and Danny ride to the rescue: in Florida, where greyhound racing thrives, they pull their rig over at racing kennels and inquire if any greyhounds are available. Here the adoption cost is nothing, but the choice is horrendous.

"So they turn loose a hundred or a hundred and fifty in a pen and say, 'Help yourself,'" says Ron.

"The longest time greyhounds make it at the track is about a year and a half," says Ron. "They are a commodity, and when they can't run fast, they are over with. We have passed mounds of dead greyhounds taller than Danny's head; they were shot at the end of the season. At the cheaper kennels, they don't even shoot them; they throw them to the alligators in the deep canals. And greyhounds make the best pets . . ."

When they are looking at one hundred greyhounds, how do they choose which ones will go home with them, I wonder. "It's a sense, a look in the eye; they put their muzzle into your hand," says Danny. "Like with horses."

The guys agree to think over the selection of dogs, say good-bye to Heather, and we head back to their neat brick rambler, a five-minute drive from their stable. It is landscaped with holly, barrels of luxuriant kalanchoe, and flower pots shaped like rabbits and pigs. A live oak sprouting with mistletoe is hung with bird feeders. The front pastures are full of retired horses, injured horses, and three handsome, leggy Thoroughbred yearlings.

From the kitchen a high voice flutes out, "Helllloooo!" Gabby, their yellow nape Amazon parrot, clambers in a large sunny cage, competing with operatic arias followed by the soundtracks of *Big River* and *Showboat* playing on the stereo. A pink fairy floats from the kitchen chandelier; cans and bags of dog food cover the counter. Under our feet, a large, confident gray tabby named Watch Kitty mingles with the pack of exuberant small dogs that race back and forth from one end of the house to the other.

Ron's other love is African wildlife, and the spacious rooms are decorated with ceramics and paintings of giraffes, zebras, and lions. There are turtle candleholders, ostrich prints, and framed photographs of Ron and Danny's dogs, their families, and their friends. The paint has been clawed off the base of the French doors leading to the dining room, where handsome portraits of their dogs are on display.

Ron comes by this love of creatures genetically. "My parents are in their late seventies, and they still go to shelters where they live in Barrington, Illinois, and adopt dogs," he says. "They adopt the geriatric cases. It's painful for them because the dogs only have a few years, but they feel older dogs will never be adopted."

Similarly, Danny's love of creatures dates back to childhood, when his mother was his co-conspirator in collecting animals. "My mother and I couldn't let it die on the road," he says. "Whatever it was, birds, turtles, anything, we were always bringing it home."

Their mercy extends to creatures small as well as great. One winter, Ron caught a mouse in their kitchen (in a live trap, of course) and was heading off to release it in the barn. "Do you know it's fourteen degrees out there?!" said Danny indignantly. He then pared down Dixie cups to make bowls for the mouse, grated Parmesan cheese, ground up pecans, and served the mouse nutritious meals until it could be released in warmer weather. "And every time we leave our Florida house, I spend twenty minutes making sure no lizards are locked in the porch," he admits.

They have been known to intercede on behalf of pet owners who need their help. They once saw an elderly man with an old rusty bike sitting on the lawn outside the Camden vet office. He was weeping, holding a bloody dog in his arms. "We asked him what's wrong," says Danny. "And he said, 'I got no money to get the vet to treat my dog.'"

So Ron marched in and told the vet clinic worker to take care of the dog and put it on his bill. The woman objected, saying, "You guys spend thousands of dollars a month here. You don't have to go taking care of other people's bills too." Then Ron, all six feet eight inches of him, threatened to sit at the clinic door until the vet attended to the dog. The vet did, Ron and Danny paid, and the dog survived.

Their frolicsome mixed-breed named Bus Stop Bobby was a gift from another man in need. "We saw a man walking outside the bus stop, and he had a little dog all matted and dirty, and we said, 'That's a cute dog,'" says Ron. "And he said, 'You want my dog?' He'd been a subcontracted laborer here, he told us, and his truck was totaled. He had to go home to Florida on the bus, which wouldn't accept his dog."

"'He a good dog, he don't shit in the house, he got his shots,' he told us," says Danny. "We offered to take the dog temporarily and arrange to get him home to Florida for the man, but he said, 'If I gotta leave him, it's only gonna be the one time.'"

So now Bobby, his short silver coat shining, romps the yard and stable, watches Ron and Danny teach lessons, and rides in their laps on the eight-hour drive between their Camden and Palm Beach homes.

There was no rescue for one of their own: Ron was teaching a class one day in Ridgeway, South Carolina, while Sunny, his Jack Russell terrier, scampered around the field. A truck pulled over and a man grabbed the friendly little dog. "I ran out of the ring, but he was gone," says Ron. "I placed an ad in the Columbia state paper with a picture, but nobody called. Finally, the truck was stopped in North Carolina by police. They found the guy had taken over forty small dogs and had sold all of them for pit-bull bait."

To comfort themselves, they recall several successes: Bessie the Bassett, Mona the Mutt, Lucky to Be Alive, and Jack the Tree Trimmer, an albino pointer who ran circles under the trees and nipped all the branches within reach. And Dottie, the bluetick hound that was so miserably sick but recovered to jubilantly eat a couch, playfully puncture every hose on the farm, and munch up three seven-hundred-dollar custom-made bridles. "But she was a sweetheart!" says Ron.

Pain, cost, and loss are worth it all, they agree. "It's what completes our hearts," says Ron. "Animals never stop giving, and without them, I'd never be entertained," says Danny.

And what about those dogs we saw at the Camden shelter? I ask. "If you step in there, you owe it to one animal at least," says Danny. "And we both stepped in there."

"We talked; we're going to go back and get the black Lab and the black-and-white one," says Ron.

"It's love: they are loving no matter how tired, dirty, exhausted, and sweaty we are," says Danny. "And we make such a small dent in the millions."

"We give back to life what we can," says Ron. "We don't drive by and assume somebody else will do it."

26

A JOY TO RAISE

PHIL MCINTYRE, HIS DOG, PRINCE, AND THEIR STAG, LI'L BUCK

"TELL ME, DO ya like fresh vegetables?" Phil McIntyre feeds wild creatures and tame creatures, and he's about to feed us. His thickly-planted garden on his lot in tiny Biscoe, North Carolina, is erupting with produce when we visit in late summer. We are here to see his orphan fawn, but first, in keeping with Southern tradition, we must be fed. "That garden 'bout worked me to death," Phil says, arranging freshly washed tomatoes and hot peppers on a tea towel in the kitchen of his small, one-storey home just beyond the freeway.

Phil's left cheek is distended by a plum-sized chew of tobacco, and he sports a gray-white goatee and neatly trimmed black hair going silver, a flat-link gold necklace and two bracelets against his deeply tanned skin, nylon shorts, deck shoes, and a T-shirt. Phil is known around Biscoe and neighboring Troy as the man who has the fawn, now a fourteen-month-old stag he named Little Buck.

"That's the dog that raised Li'l Buck," says Phil, introducing a young black Pomeranian named Prince, a lively two-year-old with long, well-groomed

Li'l Buck and a target deer meet nose to nose at Phil McIntyre's camp.

glossy hair and startlingly white teeth. His little domed forehead and limpid dark eyes make him look like a baby fur seal. "Pomeranians ain't usually black, and he's bigger 'n usual—they supposed to weigh between eight and ten pounds, but he's twenty-six pounds," Phil explains.

Phil's living room holds a tiny woodstove, a TV, and two videos (*Python* and *Road Rage*), and the wood-paneled walls are hung with a stuffed wood duck, a striped bass, and trophy heads of four of the dozens of white-tail bucks he's shot. "That's my old deer there," says Phil, referring to his trophy mounts. "I got my other deer in the [storage] container at my other place."

As the pots steam and bubble, Phil opens kitchen cupboard doors to reveal sparkling quarts of canned beans and sauerkraut made from his vegetable garden. Phil spends the day in his tiny four-room Biscoe house "doin' my cannin' and my freezin' and whatever I have to do" with Prince at his feet. He and Prince spend every night in the woods at his other property, sleeping with the buck—all in the same bed until the tiny fawn became a stag, and the stag could no longer fit safely into the bed in his camper trailer.

Phil pulls a steaming pork butt out of the roaster to cool and, while pots of vegetables simmer, sets his digital camera on the narrow kitchen counter for us, proud as a parent with home movies of his only child. It's the short and happy life of Little Buck: as a speckled fawn; nursing from a bottle, Prince slurping along with his paws balanced on the fawn's neck; dog and fawn racing across the meadow in long games of tag; Little Buck splay-legged in the first snow of his life, bucking and hopping with a young creature's joy. "He fell twice while ice skatin'," says Phil.

"I got him fourteen months ago, down at the shop [his family's welding shop]," Phil recounts as he shreds the cooling pork. "A Mexican brought him in; he didn't know what to do with him. Li'l Buck's mother got run over. He was about a day or two old. I raised him from about sixteen inches high, fed him goat milk, Carnation and water mixed together. A guy [who] used to raise deer tol' me how much to feed it. Most people give 'em too much milk. You give 'em three ounces ever' three hours and no more.

They'll drink a whole bottle, if you let 'em, and that gives them scours and kills them."

Phil's brother Gary walks into the house, a sturdy man in a baseball cap, a can of Budweiser bulging out of the breast pocket of his green T-shirt.

"Hi, Tree Monkey," Phil greets him.

"Can I borrow a bowl?" asks Gary.

"Sure, what you want it for?" says Phil.

"Cleanin' bream," says Gary. He takes the bowl onto the lawn and cleans the fish he just caught in Phil's pond with his two children, Lorie and Jacob.

When Phil is out of earshot, I ask Gary about the relationship between Little Buck and his brother.

"Lil' Buck rescued him; I can't think what he'd do without him," says Gary.

When Gary departs, we feast on yellow squash, okra, Big Boy beans, brown crowder beans, ivory ears of Silver Queen sweet corn, hot cornbread, and roast pork butt with barbecue sauce, the drippings cycled back into the succulent brown beans.

"Why Tree Monkey?" I ask Phil.

"Long time ago he went deer huntin' and he fell asleep and fell out of the tree, him and the rifle," says Phil. "It was my rifle, too, but it didn't hurt nothin'."

At his "other place," thirty-some wooded acres where Little Buck lives, Phil warns us, "I got no power or nothing, no air conditioning, just gas lanterns. It's my huntin' place. We didn't get but four over there this year. We're allowed six. There's too many does, so we try and manage it to let the bucks grow and get big."

Phil hunts with a bow and has the straight, square shoulders and posture of an archer. He also shoots turkey and deer with black powder rifles, a matter of historical interest and personal pride to him. "My great-great-grandpa, B. L. Sanders, he was the first one; he went to work for Kennedy rifle, you know those?" he says. I don't, but I know something of the weight of a black powder rifle and how hickory-hard and strong a person has to be, how steady, to hold its vast barrel, fire, and hit a deer.

After lunch, I squeeze into his Chevrolet pickup truck with Prince on the seat, packets of Red Man on the dash, a box of Milk Bones, and a .22 caliber with a hunting scope wedged between the seats. The truck bed holds a compressor, chains and saws, cantaloupes, and a gas-powered weed cutter.

"Li'l Buck used to ride around with me in the truck, layin' on the floorboards—Mama thought I was crazy," Phil explains. "When Li'l Buck would try to get up on the seat, Prince, he'd grab his legs and make him lay back down."

We stop briefly at Mama's house, a spacious suburban rambler reached via a wooden covered bridge over a large fish pond. After we feed the fish, Phil's half-brother Lewis hands us five pounds of blueberries freshly picked from an enormous bush behind the home.

The town of Biscoe is sleepy and blue collar, and its business consists largely of textile mills, foundries, and auto salvage. Signs indicate a prison down the road. Generous gardens bloom adjacent to homes set in woods drowning in spires of kudzu along roadsides, where magnolias with stiff glossy leaves flourish. There are churches, some little more than concrete bunkers with crude spires, and houses lost in trumpet vines and fields of Shasta daisies. Street signs and businesses bear old English, Scottish, and Irish names: Thigpen, Hunycutt, Tillery, and McBee.

Phil steers the pickup into the woods, opening and closing a metal barrier gate hung with "No Hunting" signs. The signs notwithstanding, this is a hunting community and one that doesn't necessarily follow orders. I am worried that Phil's Little Buck will fall to a poacher in here. "I got government land all around me; you can't gun-hunt in there," he explains. And any archers would presumably be close enough to see Little Buck's two bright orange collars that indicate he is somebody's pet, he adds.

A quarter-mile into the woods, the dirt road circles before an old brown-and-white trailer supported on concrete blocks. There's a tidy wooden outhouse, two hammocks, a picnic table sheltered by a tarpaulin, and porch swings under the pines. The ground is covered with pine needles, bones, beer bottle caps, empty cartridge shells from Phil's target range, deer droppings, and loose blossom-like balls of Phil's discarded tobacco. A much-punctured target deer stands in the field behind the trailer.

"Li'l Buck!" Phil calls. "Li'l Buck!" Within minutes, a tiny young stag materializes, tail down and not the least frightened. Kingly in his carriage, with large round black eyes, he has a moist nose, exquisite small black hooves, and pipestem legs, slightly cow-hocked in back. Two blaze-orange collars hang around his slender neck, and his antlers are covered in rich, slate-gray velvet.

"He's not but a year and two months old," says Phil, handing a cookie to Little Buck, whose mouth has upturned corners, giving his muzzle the appearance of a silent smile. He is a light sorrel color, his back not quite as high as my waist. Phil estimates Little Buck's weight at eighty-five pounds and says that should double by next year.

"You in paradise here," says Phil, seated at the picnic table, slicing cucumbers, cantaloupe, and apples and handing them one by one to Little Buck, who serenely munches them. He throws in a few oatmeal cookies, peanuts, and four dog biscuits and pours a stream of dry kibble into a wooden deer feeder with a mineral block.

"These are Li'l Buck's first antlers; last year he was a 'knot head' we call it or 'button buck.' I keep him fed good. He has good protein—dog biscuits and cow peas."

I pick up the only reading material here, a rain-dappled copy of the *Whitetail News* lying on the picnic table, and open it to a dog-eared article: "Cause and Effects of 200 Days of Antler Growth."

In the living room of Phil's trailer, more mounted buck heads hang on the walls, and in the bedroom, still another buck is on display, his ten-point rack in seemingly perilous proximity to the small bed. Everything is neat, orderly, and still. Through the open bedroom door, a bobwhite calls in the woods.

"I tell you what, I got cable TV, and when deer shows come on, that dad-blessed dog watches 'em," says Phil, as Prince stands on his hind legs, thoroughly washing the buck's ears with his tongue. "Li'l Buck, he's my buddy," he says, taking a dog brush first to the deer and then to Prince, who pants with pleasure. "One time he got his leg through his collar, and I tried to get his leg out, and me and him hit the ground. He tore my pants off. My butt was black and blue. And that lump on the antler is where he got caught in the hammock and just panicked."

"What's the drill?" Phil asks Prince, who promptly sits. "Be easy now." Prince delicately takes a morsel of cookie from Phil's hand.

I reach toward the buck, who sniffs me carefully, then allows me to touch his antlers. They are hot and hard, alive under the velvet, about the circumference of bicycle handlebars. I stroke his face and scratch his ears, which leaves a slightly greasy feeling on my hands, like lanolin from sheep's wool.

"I'm fixin' to build a house here and a great big pond over there," says Phil, pointing to where a spring runs between recently cleared slopes planted with cow peas and white clover for deer and turkeys.

"He got more to eat than by god I got to eat," says Phil, rubbing Little Buck's head. The buck pushes against him like a happy cat enjoying the caresses.

"Come on, boy, let's git!" says Phil, walking off with Prince for a post-prandial stroll.

Phil used to be the superintendent for a construction company, where, he says, he made good money and liked the work. A few months before we met him, the numbness he had been feeling in his hands and feet while riding his ATV was diagnosed as diabetes. He switched from junk food to vegetables and venison and plummeted from 210 to 170 pounds. He looks healthy and fit, but the peripheral neuropathy that comes with the disease means he's not supposed to drive a car, truck, or ATV more than fifteen minutes at a stretch, which limits his ability to work. And through a glitch in unemployment and disability law, he says, "The heck of it is, I don't get no money."

We walk through a forest of shortleaf pine, oak, slick hickory, and sweet gum. Little Buck stops to browse, then canters to catch up.

If work and health have gone badly, love has gone worse for Phil. "I'm single right now, and I'm gonna stay that way too," he says. The previous year, his second wife left him after what Phil says was a dispute about money and fidelity complicated by antagonistic stepdaughters. Two weeks before our visit, she served him with divorce papers.

"I had a rough time," he says, his eyes full of sorrow. "I was kind of lost. They brought me back," he says, indicating Prince and Little Buck. "They were my salvation. Li'l Buck, he been a joy to raise."

How can Phil love Little Buck and kill his kin? What's the difference, I wonder, between the deer he loves and the deer he shoots and eats? "It's just different; he's a special thing," says Phil. "The other ones I'm not attached to. I still like to hunt, and he goes huntin' with me. When I'm on the deer stand, he lays down under the stand. If I'm on the ground, he lays down 'side of me. He's been right there when I hang 'em on the chain and dress 'em out."

The five of us—dog, deer, man, and women—walk across swales of cow peas and white clover into the woods, where a yard-high wall of woven brush and a bench provide a blind for watching and hunting deer and turkeys.

"The other day, me and Li'l Buck set down in the turkey blind, and turkeys came in here not ten feet away—I got 'em on video," says Phil. "Deer, turkeys, it don't make no difference; they love that white clover."

He sometimes goes to Texas to hunt deer, Phil explains, but he "wasn't going to Texas to kill a doggone turkey. I got bigger turkeys here than they got."

In the shade behind the clearing for Phil's future dream house, a wild tom turkey, the last of fifteen chicks he raised, pecks and paces in a pen, and a Rhode Island Red rooster and hens laze in another. The doors to a semi-sized metal storage trailer stand open, revealing furniture, an old stereo, deer hides, a dusty, stuffed red tail hawk, floor lamps, and a half-dozen mounted buck heads tumbled in different positions.

Phil has always cared for wild things. He had a screech owl, raccoons, and squirrels as a child and is possibly the only person to be cited by a police officer for reckless driving caused by a raccoon crawling around on his lap.

He's healing in these woods, walking shirtless and barelegged for a raging case of psoriasis, and taking a shoebox full of medications for the arthritis chewing his bones, the high blood pressure, and, maybe, the depression. "My life went all to hell," Phil reflects.

The saving element in all of his recent pain is his young deer. "He's my little buddy; he don't talk no trash to me. And he don't know he's a deer. Except for Li'l Buck and the dog, I got nobody to be in charge of."

"I want me another one; it's still not too late this year," says Phil. "I'd like to have me a doe next time. I'd like to see what the difference is. I don't know what I'd do without Li'l Buck. I guess I'd be crazy."

Tory the mustang was born with crippled hooves and will never be ridden. He lives at an Arizona ranch designed for children with handicaps that has many handicapped animals as well.

27

WHISPERING HOPE

DIANE REID AND WHISPERING HOPE RANCH

SQUALLS OF SLEET spatter across the rimrock above us, sending veils of snow mist onto a pasture of orange poppies as our jeep clatters across the cattle guard. At the far end of the pasture, the scent of lodgepole and Ponderosa pine needles mingles with apple blossoms blooming near an ancient log cabin. Beyond the cabin, three donkeys nibble on iris shoots by a pond where a willow tree leans above a stream. Eeyore, a large gray donkey, and two miniature donkeys named Cuddles and Kisses snuffle and chew and consider the day in this quiet hour before the children arrive.

"Eeyore's just the best guy," says Diane Reid, who has come out of the cabin office to meet us. Diane is the founder of Whispering Hope Ranch, here in the mountains east of Payson, Arizona. Like many animals at the ranch, Eeyore has physical challenges. Before he arrived, Eeyore had a condition in his hind feet that limited his mobility, Diane explains.

"He knows exactly why he's here and what he's doing. Thank you, Eeyore," she says, as his black velvet nose busses her cheek in a donkey smooch. What Eeyore does is greet children who have challenges also, children born with physical differences or who suffered illness, injury, emotional trauma or have developmental disabilities.

Now this nineteenth-century working ranch is being transformed into a twenty-first-century ranch that can accommodate those with special needs, and Eeyore is one of the staff. Diane walks with us up a path to where a new A-frame log cabin has just been completed. It's a prototype for a dozen more cabins, each designed with special lighting, drains for dialysis, and wheelchair-accessible bathrooms. There will be an arena where the campers—kids with spina bifida, epilepsy, autism, and hemophilia—can ride some of the ranch horses. But most of all, there are animals of all sizes, ages, and conditions, animals who know what it's like to be different, in peril, injured or abandoned.

"Several years ago, when I went through a divorce, animals were healers for me," says Diane, who has filled the forty-five acres with a hundred rescued creatures ranging from Sandy the emu, to J.T. the miniature mule, to City Kitty, a formerly feral cat from Manhattan. Now she and the board members are raising more than nine million dollars to fund a camp where animals serve as emotional and physical healers for children.

"Whispering Hope, that's from a hymn I learned as a child; it's about angels and healing," Diane explains. "The idea of the ranch is that people can be with animals with similar kinds of trauma and physical difficulties— that can be powerfully healing."

Children, aides, teachers, and parents swarm onto the ranch drive, being lowered from buses with special power lifts for wheelchairs. There are children with severe scars or missing limbs, kids with cerebral palsy, and one little girl with a cranial-facial injury.

Taurie, a pale blonde mustang, noses at them and at us, demanding scratches. His front hooves torque inward in unnatural curves, like a pair of outsized fortune cookies. Taurie was born without coffin bones—the core of the hoof—perhaps the result of his mother's malnutrition during pregnancy. Diane bought Pisces, his mother, at a "killer" auction, an auction where horses are sold by the pound for meat.

"She looked like she was dying when I met her," says Diane, as we pet the mare, now roving the pasture with her son. "She was all bones and standing with her head down, starved. It looked like she wasn't gonna make it, but I purchased her on the spot. When the vet checked her, we found out she was in foal and due imminently."

Taurie is seven now, walking well despite his twisted feet. He carries himself in a self-confident, even cocky way and runs in the meadow, kicking up his back feet in delight.

"I want this to be a healing place for both people and animals," says Diane. "The hard part is we get calls every week about animals that need to be here or they will be put to sleep."

City Kitty was one of the hundred lucky ones. He came from a colony of wild cats in New York City. "Someone tried to poison them all, and a woman rescued the four who survived," Diane explains. "She got them spayed, neutered, and vaccinated, but she couldn't place him. He had an eyelid that turned under. The eye ran all the time, so nobody wanted him. She called us and asked if he could come here to live, and since she wanted to see the ranch anyway, she brought him out."

City Kitty arrived on a snowy March day and promptly went into hiding, emerging in August at the renovated ranch house office. "He was just sitting on the porch, as if to say, 'Where have you been?'" says Diane, as the cat escorts us around the grounds. "It took us weeks to be able to touch him."

His friends are Sweet Pea, a fainting goat; Ferdinand, a miniature Brahma steer; and a fallow deer named Cupid, all refugees from a roadside petting zoo. "The animals were in a twelve-by-twelve pen, and they were harassed by kids, and nobody took care of them," she says. "I got a phone call that the steer, deer, and goat were going to be done away with, 'Unless you can take them. And we have to know by Friday.' This was Wednesday. These little animals had been friends since they were babies."

Now Ferdinand lives with Chili Bean the big Holstein. Since Sweet Pea is fragile and subject to falls, she lives with two goats named Billi and Vanilli and with Buckwheat, a horned white cashmere goat with a severe side bite and a tongue that dangles out to the side.

As Diane gathers animals and children, she increases her staff: an events coordinator, someone to manage the camp and office, and two full-time animal caretakers, who live in the new ranch house with the long porches. Members of the hourly animal staff live down the valley, while Mary Clark, executive director of Whispering Hope Ranch, has two part-time staffers at the office in Scottsdale. (Mary was not an animal lover before coming to the Ranch. "I used to pet animals through my sleeve," she confesses. "Now I kiss llamas on the nose, and I have a rescued poodle.")

A rooster and four black hens peck and flutter in a chicken yard near the goat pen.

"We call them Pokey and the Buddhist Hens—they're a rock group," says Diane. "He was a single rooster from the nearby Buddhist monastery, and he didn't know how to be a rooster at first. "

"You dance, don't you? Do the Hokey Pokey," she asks. And the rooster obediently does a spin and drops a wing, spins, ducks, and drops the other wing.

Diane scoops up Pokey and cuddles him. Pokey chirps and murmurs, tipping his head side to side, considering the situation. She offers him to a physically challenged girl being driven in a golf cart to visit the chickens, but the girl wants no part of the rooster. Diane persists, "Oh, he's talking to you!" she says, as the brightly feathered rooster hums and chirps.

We straggle on, kids on foot and in wheelchairs, mothers, and City Kitty with his tail in the air, up a rise to the stable to visit Lucky Lady, a small white Arabian mare. When she was two, she pulled away from her trainer, flipped backwards and struck her head. Now the mare is blind, but she uses her whiskers like a cat to sense her surroundings, the stable walls, the stall door, and the hands stretched out to touch her porcelain-fine face.

A boy named Jonothan glows and coos at Lucky Lady, who snuffles at his hands. He suffers from two types of muscular dystrophy, and when he also developed Kearn-Sayers syndrome, a rare congenital disorder, he started to lose his vision and has difficulty walking. He is now in a wheelchair, which a friend has rolled into the stable aisle.

Diane was exposed to the magnetism and power of horses growing up in Twin Falls, southern Idaho, where her father raised and trained Thoroughbreds. "My brothers and sisters had horses too," she recalls, "but as a child, I was never really comfortable on horses; I was nervous about them. So I had a crow, a lamb, and a rooster."

Only as an adult and after a divorce did she learn to ride, Diane admits. Her first mount was a three-year-old mare named Sheba. "I was in situations with her and was amazed by her. We rode past snakes and everything. Our rides were magical! After I moved up here, I rode for awhile, but as I started really listening to animals, I started to see we humans use animals for our own benefit, and in many cases it is harmful or hurtful. Riding started to feel like the wrong thing to me."

"We humans buy and sell horses and train them, and if they can't do it, like the *Black Beauty* story, they are taken away from their friends (and they *do* have friends, both human and animal) and from their homes," she says. "Often they are treated in ways I'd never want any animal to be treated. I am not going to change the world, but I chose not to ride any more. We do drive a carriage here, and the children can ride, but I personally chose not to do those things."

Diane's hopeful herd of one hundred, give or take a few, includes five enormous emus, a pair of turkeys named Butterball and Tom, a quartet of fallow deer named Comet, Cupid, Prancer, and Dancer, and a dozen ducks, some of them blind from toxic chemicals. "They are so fascinating to watch. They didn't go into 'Oh dear, I'm blind'—they just figure it out and go on," she insists. "For animals, it's the same when people treat them badly. They say, 'Oh well, I still love you.'"

"I always pick the turkeys to talk about; they know their names, and they come when I call them," she says. "I kiss them; they sit on my lap and talk back to me."

The summer after she rescued Butterball and Tom, Diane was conducting a seminar on the barn porch, and Butterball waddled all the way up to the barn, sat down smack in the circle of people and went to sleep. "She was so funny, and it is a long hard walk up that big hill on those little turkey legs," Diane giggles.

The ranch is a great leap from where Diane has spent most of her life. She earned a teaching degree in public safety and a master's degree in environmental health and community medicine, and she worked in the oil service industry, as a director of marketing and human resources director, and traveled the world. "I was always very busy and goal-oriented, but I knew there was this other way to be," she explains. It took a divorce and a job change to bring her into a quieter realm. "I wished I could create a special place where people would come and feel loved, a place they could be away from everything that felt bad in their lives," she says. At Whispering Hope, she has begun to offer that.

"The last fifteen years or so have been about spiritual transformation, learning about myself, letting go of my fears and critical attitudes. I finally got it, at least most of the time—how to be in the moment, nonjudgmental, and loving."

In other words, she aspires to be pretty much like Eeyore, Butterball, and Lucky Lady. "Animals are so sweet; they have no judgment," says Diane. "I used to be a perfectionist, cleaning, working, and worrying. Now I love my life; it is so joyful."

28

SPEAKING UP FOR CASSIDY

RANDI GOLUB AND HER CATS

CASSIDY THE CAT was one needle-prick away from eternal sleep when a bold decision stopped the procedure. The young gray-and-cream cat, whose hind leg had been shattered by a .22 caliber bullet, was full of fleas, half-starved, and reeking, and a second bullet was lodged close to his spine. The veterinary staff at the Eugene, Oregon, animal hospital had decided the best thing to do was euthanize what they figured was a hopelessly injured feral cat.

Randi Golub was head veterinary technician, and it was her job to administer the tranquilizer that precedes the fatal injection. She had done that, but as she spoke to the cat and stroked his scraggly coat, he purred and licked her hand. "The injection was drawn, the vet was standing there with it, but something about this cat got to me. He just didn't feel feral. I felt so sad—and I felt we should try to save him," says Randi.

Randi, who does in-home nursing care for cats, as well as boarding and hospice care for them, had seen thousands of cats in varying stages of distress. "I could never stand doing euthanasia unless it was the right thing, and I felt this was not the right thing. The second question that popped up in my mind right then was, 'Who is going to be responsible for him?' We can't save him and then leave him to spend his life in a cage," says Randi. In that instant, she turned to the vet and asked her to halt the euthanasia. She took responsibility for Cassidy, and she has never regretted it.

Randi and her husband, John, share a 1961 bungalow that is half-hidden behind mounds of lavender on a quiet street near the Willamette River. Randi's station wagon is parked in the driveway, its rear window advertising her services as a cat nurse and cat hospice provider.

Chuck, a gray tabby with a weight lifter's build, chirrups a welcome to me at the door, and Q-tip, a one-eyed white rat, greets me with a nip on the finger through the bars of her cage. A stunted black female cat named Mini skitters playfully across the linoleum, and wide-eyed, elderly Kringle ("The most annoying cat I ever met," laughs Randi. "He won't leave you alone") attaches himself to my side.

Cool, rainy Eugene is known for being the town where the sixties went after the sixties were over, but this home is strictly warm, sunny pre–World War II Florida—pastel yellow and periwinkle walls, framed vintage beach art, woven rattan furniture upholstered in 1940s tropical foliage fabrics, and floors of speckled linoleum. Quiet jazz—Billie Holiday and Stefan Grappelli—trickles through the rooms.

Randi is a youthful, middle-aged woman, short and motherly with close-cropped blonde hair and deep-set eyes behind narrow glasses. Gold cat-head earrings flash at her earlobes. Cats pose on the kitchen counter, two play under the sofa, another dances down the hall—but I notice that the house is astonishingly clean and odor-free. "Thirteen cats is not a number I recommend for anyone," Randi concedes. "And I won't say it isn't tiring, but they give back so much to us that it's easy for me."

She calls to Cassidy, who rises from a fluffy blue cat bed on the floor near

Cassidy lost a hind leg, but he now inspires and brings comfort to senior citizens, children, and people in hospices. He helps teach compassion to everyone he meets.

a bookcase, his gait a curious combination of scoot and hop. Despite his missing back leg, he manages to get up on my lap, fix me with his topaz blue eyes, and mark my chin with his cheeks. He has large, lynx-like gray ears, and a coat of cream patches alternating with gray tabby stripes—possibly a combination of Siamese and domestic shorthair. There is no stump to his left hind leg; it simply isn't there. A small white tuft marks the scar along his lower spine where the second bullet was removed. I stroke his throat, Cassidy purrs blissfully, and soon the air is full of white fur that settles on my black jeans and turtleneck.

Saving Cassidy required a team effort beginning with Brooks Fahy, an animal lover who had noticed the stray cat. He followed a trail of blood, put on fireplace gloves, and crawled under a porch to retrieve him.

"We saved his amputated leg with the gunshot," Randi explains, holding an X-ray up to the light from the large patio doors in her living room. A ghostly constellation of lead bits gleam along the delicate, crushed feline femur. "We know who the person is who shot him. She lives in a rural area about half an hour from Eugene, and when we questioned her, she admits she shot *at* him, but we don't have the time and money to prosecute her."

After Randi's eleventh-hour decision, another veterinarian volunteered to amputate the leg and remove the second bullet. "The worst was the seizures afterwards," says Randi. "He couldn't hold his head up or walk. We had to hold him up in the litter box; we had to hold his head for him to eat or drink."

For the first week, Cassidy needed twenty-four-hour care; several vet techs, a veterinarian, and Brooks Fahy each took him home for a couple of nights and stayed up nursing him. Then he needed to relearn to walk. "When I first put him on the grass for traction, it broke my heart—he tried so hard, but he couldn't stand," says Randi. As Cassidy became stronger, Randi rigged a bath towel and a cat harness to suspend him like a puppet. She placed mats against the walls of the rooms and towed him around, steadying the three-legged cat as he regained strength and grappled with his altered sense of balance. Over a month, he taught himself how to walk again, going from the harness to leaning against the walls for support, she explains. "He had tremors, but through the whole thing, he was purring and loving and licking my hand. He is the most loving cat."

In September 2007, Cassidy passed his Delta Society test, becoming one of a few hundred cats in the country to be a registered pet partner. (Delta Society is a Washington State–based international nonprofit organization that improves human health through service and therapy animals.) The test involves a physical exam and a temperament test to determine how the animal reacts to new people and noisy or strange situations. Now Cassidy and Randi go to assisted-living homes, where Cassidy brings out the best in human beings.

Cassidy provided an opportunity for Randi to take a lifetime responsibility for a needy creature, and she didn't hesitate. But he's not her only inspiring dependent creature.

"Jimmy Jam! Come on, Jimmy!" Randi calls. A slender orange kitten bounds out of an adjoining room, a delicate youngster with a long muzzle, outsized ears, and distinctive butterscotch whorls along his sides. He scampers around to nose Cassidy, who has settled down in a tiny blue tent, one of a dozen cat beds in the living room. Then Jimmy strolls over to select a catnip-stuffed mouse from a basket of toys. When I pick him up and cuddle him, colorless sutures abruptly poke me in the face—the kitten's eyelids have recently been sewn shut.

"He's blind," Randi confirms. "He was a stray with terrible eye infections, and we hoped to save one eye, but we couldn't. If you didn't know, you could barely tell he can't see."

I put Jimmy down and he darts off to wrestle with a beaded curtain hanging in the doorway between the kitchen and laundry room, while Randi shows me the wider part of her feline realm. "This is my WiFi cat-fé. I can take my laptop outdoors here," she says, parting the sliding doors and leading the way through a fenced garden that encircles three-quarters of her bungalow. "At the end of December, we only get about six hours of daylight around here, so I'm out here as often as I can be."

The yard contains a huge southern magnolia, a cluster of Oregon's

Someone shot Cassidy twice, but cat nurse Randi Golub of Eugene, Oregon, saved his life.

omnipresent rhododendrons, pink-red camellia buds already unfurling in the February chill, and an herb garden with rosemary and lavender. Tiki torches surround the garden.

If Randi is the local cat whisperer, she says, laughing, then John is a "car whisperer" who diagnoses high-end autos—but he's also a big softie. "My husband is a real motorhead, but he loves the cats—he's the one who instituted a tiki-torch ceremony when we bury a cat here. He leaves the torches on all night for them."

Randi has other ways of honoring her late customers. "One year, five of my clients' cats passed away, so I planted three hundred bulbs—tulips, crocuses, lilies—as a memorial to them. And we hold a celebration of life, a garden party, and people bring photos of their animals. I like to find ways to deal with sadness and channel it constructively. This year I planted four hundred bulbs."

Beyond a fish pond (guarded from great blue herons by a toy figure of Godzilla) is an arched roof housing a shady cat run with ramps, toys, and towers. Finches flit in the shade of a massive, deep green deodar tree that shelters a yellow one-room cottage with blue shutters and white trellises. The interior is beyond spotless, with blue counters, two skylights, air filters, an aquarium, and fish mobiles. The cottage holds a maximum of four cats; each kennel has an outdoor run, a bed and chair, toys, and lace curtains. Today the foursome includes Teddi, a sixteen-year-old that was once hit by a car and needs to have her bladder expressed daily, and Sparky, an asthmatic cat that travels with his own inhaler. Their owners are on vacation, and they have entrusted their fragile darlings to Randi. "I am booked here for the next two years—especially Thanksgiving, Christmas, and summers," she says. "I really wouldn't trust anybody else to do this. And people are so appreciative and grateful."

Being a full-time cat caretaker—whether it's Cassidy and Jimmy or her clients' cats—means very little downtime for Randi. She is literally captive to her cats, held hostage by their needs and her big heart. Fortunately for her, "Nothing fires me up like working with animals," she says. "I got this animal thing from Dad. He'd come home from work, and his greatest joy was to have our two Siamese cats sleep on his big belly. Dad sold floor coverings, and to this day I can't have a scrap of carpet in the house, which is a good thing considering the life we live."

She grew up in Pennsylvania, the youngest of four children, and holds degrees in animal-center management and veterinary technology. Until a few months before she met Cassidy, Randi had a Siamese cat named Violet that visited reservations, nursing homes, hospices, schools, and libraries with her. And Cassidy has succeeded Violet. "It's a way for people to get their hands on a warm, furry, loving body," she says. "I see people in their wheelchairs off by themselves, isolated, but with a cat there, they begin to share their lives and they talk—maybe about the animals they had when they were eight years old. They can't remember what they had for breakfast, but they can tell me about their puppy."

Cassidy revives their love of life by demonstrating his own joyful personality, Randi believes. "Some things are more difficult for him because of his physical condition, but he's the happiest creature I've ever seen. Sometimes I watch him sleeping in the sun on his back, and I feel so lucky that I was somehow there when he needed me. And I also feel fortunate that I listened to myself, that I spoke up."

Randi and John have not had a vacation for more than two years. Nonetheless, she describes herself as feeling blessed. "Cassidy has transformed my life, because he's a living, twenty-four-hour-a-day reminder of how you can overcome any kind of physical or emotional obstacle, and learn how to trust," says Randi. "It would have been easy for him to withdraw, to be scared and not trust people, but even while he went through pain, he was loving and trusting. He reminds me on a daily basis what trust is all about."

"I can tell he's grateful for everything I've done for him, but I'm the one who is immensely grateful."

ACKNOWLEDGMENTS

THANKS TO THE following kindhearted and extraordinary people, without whom this book would not have been possible: Cathryn Andrews and Norton Stillman of Nodin Press, who inspired and fostered the book from the beginning. They share our lifelong tenderness towards animals and our sense of obligation to help them. The lovely and photogenic Kimberly Carlson and her charming goldendoodle, Chloe, for modeling for us. Barbara Baugnon at the Oregon Humane Society was a tremendous help with our three Oregon stories. Bill Dorn and Bill Hammond, who guided us throughout this project. And our wise and patient editor, Renée Sedliar.

Our deep gratitude to Dr. Jane Goodall and Dr. Temple Grandin, two of the busiest people on the planet, who both saw fit to take the time to read our book and graciously provide a foreword and preface, respectively.

To all the subjects in the book. It was a privilege to spend time with these kind people and their animal companions.

—KARIN WINEGAR AND JUDY OLAUSEN

KARIN WINEGAR wishes to thank the following: Peter Moore for his support and patience. The wise, funny, and gifted team of Jacquie Trudeau and Renée Fredrickson; the members of the Monday group (Mindy, Stu, Theresa, Teresa, Carey, Michael, Jeff, Ed, Jim, and Shirley); and Nancy and Mike McAllister, Allie Hamilton, John and Betsy Phillips, Sara Grace, and Bill Ersland, who know what it means to rescue and be rescued. Thanks as well to Joan Ericksen and Peter Lancaster for their generous professional advice; to neighbors Felicia Spivey and Tony Buettner for their lead to Phil the deer man; to John Sherman for the lead to Don and Lillian; and to Nevada Barr for introducing us to Elton and PeeWee and letting me sleep on her sofa with her darling dogs.

The animals throughout my life who made it worth living, including but not limited to: Rudy, Heidi, Bruni, Venus, Cupid, Zuma, Wendy, Peter, Mitty, Molly, Filly, Sugar, Silver, Mr. Smith, Licorice Bit, Chocolate Bit, Caramel Cat, Kitkat, Romeo, Summer, Wheatie, Shadow, Houdini, Bill, Chico, Sam, Dude, Marquis, Blaze, Prinz, Smokey, Bailey, and Mine Too. And my long-suffering parents, Deanne and Wally Winegar, who delivered many animals to me and tolerated the ones I brought home.

My thanks to the indisputably gifted Judy Olausen, who could have been doing emotionally easier and more profitable work in her studio but instead chose to join me in this cross-country adventure of the heart.

And above all, my gratitude to Gabe, who rescued me from the day he was born until he handed me off to others and went over the rainbow bridge.

—KW

JUDY OLAUSEN wishes to thank the following people for their lifelong friendship, help, and total support that went above and beyond, especially while working on the stories in their area:

Barb and Jim Quale for their help plus room and board on the Sheriff Joe Arpaio story.

Carol and David Fisher for their help securing the Randy Grim story. Randy, Carol, and David will single-handedly save St. Louis.

Judy Fesenmaier and Brian Williams, Shirajoy Abry and Art Christofferson, Kelly Hayes, the Fingermans, Ruth Godfrey, Brent Marmo, Tom Murtha, Betsy Sedio, Raleigh Wolpert, and Dr. Schuneman.

To my husband, Brian Sundstrom, for his kindness, grace, understanding, and patience. No one could ask for a more perfect life-mate.

Thank you to my amazingly talented, award-winning coauthor and collaborator, Karin Winegar, whom I have had the privilege of working with for many years. Our first assignment included dinner with the Prince and Princess of Wales, Charles and Diana. A very good start to years of working together. Now her passionate commitment to animal issues is an inspiration to me and all who meet her.

My little angel Tuffy, who died in my arms and was in my heart all during this book project.

—JO

CHLOE THE GOLDENDOODLE (a cross of golden retriever and poodle) was purchased from a Wisconsin breeder by a family in Minneapolis, Minnesota. She is now owned by Kimberly and Ron Carlson and their children, Spencer and Mackenzie, who live on a fourteen-acre hobby farm in Wayzata, Minnesota.

"The family had five children including two sets of twins who went to preschool with our kids," Kimberly explains. "And when we moved to a hobby farm, we still had our kids in preschool together. They came in every day with their puppy and we oohed and ahhed at her. But when their puppy was seven months old, the mother called me and said, 'That's it! I am either destroying the dog or sending it to the humane society. She's deaf, she won't obey, she rolls in her poop every day, and I just can't do it anymore.'"

The Carlsons already had two standard poodles, but Kimberly called Ron and asked, "Can we do one more dog?" He said, "Definitely," and so the family brought Chloe to their home.

Chloe—now "CC" for Chloe Carlson—joined their two poodles, Coco and Chanel. "She peed and pooped and chewed everything—not furniture, fortunately—and she carries things in her mouth, and she piddles when you greet her at the door," says Kimberly. "But she's so endearing. And the best thing is that Ronnie has fallen in love with her."

Chloe, with her black wells of eyes framed by two-inch-long eyelashes and her sweet, obliging personality, was never deaf, according to the

Carlsons' veterinarian. She just chose not to listen to her previous family. "When the family comes over to visit her, we tell the kids the poodles have made her better, and she can hear now," says Kimberly.

And for her part, Chloe clings to her family. "She is so funny, so absolutely, endearingly wonderful," says Kimberly. "The kids adore her so; she's heartwarming and makes us laugh."

The Carlson household includes six horses (four of them adopted from Minnesota Hooved Animal Rescue—see page 59); four llamas named Versace, Pucci, Prada, and Calvin; and five cats (three of them rescued). "It's a drop in the bucket, but somebody has to do it," says Kimberly, who once diverted oncoming semitrucks on a highway to rescue a gray kitten. The cat, which they named Freeway, is devoted to her.

"I think the ones that are rescued know it," says Kimberly. "We made a difference in theirs lives, and they are so appreciative of us."

RESOURCES AND ORGANIZATIONS

THE FOLLOWING IS a list of the organizations featured in this book, including links to their Web sites. In addition, we have provided URLs for two national animal welfare organizations that have local branches.

FEATURED ORGANIZATIONS

CHAPTER 6

The Maricopa County Sheriff's Office Animal Safe Hospice
www.mcso.org

CHAPTER 7

Virginia Voters for Animal Welfare
www.virginiavotersforanimalwelfare.com

CHAPTER 10

Minnesota Hooved Animal Rescue Foundation
www.mnhoovedanimalrescue.org

CHAPTER 11

Pegasus Riding Academy for the Handicapped
www.pegasusridingacademy.org

NATIONAL ANIMAL WELFARE ORGANIZATIONS

The Humane Society of the United States
www.hsus.org

The American Society for the Prevention of
Cruelty to Animals
www.aspca.org